AF614451

To Bear Witness

By Hal Shearon McBride, Jr.

Copyright © 2009
By Hal Shearon McBride, Jr.
ISBN: 9780557044443

Published by Lulu, Inc.
Raleigh, NC
www.lulu.com

TO BEAR WITNESS

"If it's true that our collective past exists inside all of us, unless we take the time to bear witness to the best of those who strived before us, our chance to learn from their lives will be lost forever, and we will be the poorer for it."

Mark Frost
The Match

Hal Shearon McBride, Jr.

A Memoir

To Billie Jean:
The love of my life; for her unyielding support
And still one of "those pretty little Martin girls".

PRINCIPAL CHARACTERS

Bankhead, Roy "Dad" – Close friend of James H. McBride and Publisher of the Haskell County Tribune.

Calhoun, Opal – Classroom teacher in the Stigler Elementary School (Boone School) and Aunt to Jon Edward Conard.

Claunts, Hubert (1894 to 1990) – Husband to Vivian Pearl Lane Claunts, Father to Hubert "Boots" Claunts and Rupert (John) "Tag" Claunts, Uncle to the author and co-owner of the Stigler 5 & Up.

Claunts, Hubert Bluford "Boots" (1919-) – Eldest son of Vivian Lane Claunts and Hubert Claunts, Cousin to the author.

Claunts, Rupert (Changed to John) Wesley "Tag" (1920-1992) – Youngest son of Vivian Lane Claunts and Hubert Claunts, Cousin to the author.

Claunts, Vivian Pearl (Lane) (1902 to 1966) – Wife to Hubert Claunts, Mother to H. B. "Boots" Claunts and J. W. "Tag" Claunts, Eldest sister to Follie Belle (Lane) McBride, Aunt to author and co-owner of Stigler 5 & Up.

Conard, Jon Edward – Childhood neighbor and friend of the author.

Conklin, Thomas, D.O. – A lifetime of service to Stigler, Oklahoma as a Physician.

Cooper, George – Longtime City of Stigler law enforcement officer.

Cundiff, Anna Lee (McBride) – Youngest daughter of James H. and Annie Gorman McBride, wife to Ellsworth Cundiff and Aunt to the author.

Cundiff, Ellsworth – Husband to Anna Lee McBride, retired Lt. Cornel (U.S. Army) and retired Professor, University of Georgia and Uncle to the author. (Uncle Elic)

Fisher, James – Boyhood friend of the author.

Hargis, W.D. – Insurance agent whose office was located above the television shop of H. Shearon McBride in Stigler, Oklahoma, Gold Star Father and mentor to my brother.

Hays, A. W. – Business associate of J. H. McBride and resident of Muskogee, Oklahoma.

Gibson, Clem – Salesman for Hays and Buchanan Dry Goods Company.

Grubbs, W. G. "Bill" – Salesman for Hays and Buchanan Dry Goods Company.

Jack, Bob – Husband to Johnnie Jack, Huntington, Arkansas farmer, close personal friend of James Howett and Annie McBride.

Jack, Johnnie – Wife to Bob Jack, Huntington, Arkansas.

James, Paul – Husband to Elnora James, Father to Jimmy James, co-owner of Oklahoma Tire and Supply, Stigler, Oklahoma, and companion with Shearon McBride in first television venture.

James, Elnora – Wife to Paul James, Father to Jimmy James and co-owner of Oklahoma Tire and Supply, Stigler, Oklahoma.

Lane, Archie Jimmy (1908 to 1911) – Son of O.B. and Marvella Lane.

Lane, Follie Belle – See Follie Belle McBride.

Lane, Julius Breckinridge "Jack" (1928 to -) – Son of Lacy

Lane and Cousin to the author.

Lane, Lacy Leo (1905 to 1935) – Son of O.B. and Marvella Lane; Father of Jack Lane.

Lane, Marvella Hammock (1882 to 1978) – Wife of Oscar Breckinridge Lane, Mother of Vivian Lane, Lacy Leo Lane, Ruth Lane, Archie Jimmy Lane and Follie Belle Lane and maternal Grandmother to the author (Mema Lane and Mrs. O.B. Lane).

Lane, Oscar Breckinridge (1882 to 1938) – Husband of Marvella Hammock Lane, Father of Vivian Lane, Lacy Lane, Ruth Lane, Archie Lane and Follie Belle Lane and maternal Grandfather to the author.

Lane (Nicodemus, Grace, Lightfoot), Ruth – daughter of O.B. Lane and Marvella Lane.

Lane, Vivian Pearl – See Vivian Pearl Claunts.

Martin, Billie Jean – See Billie Jean McBride.

McBride, Anna Lee – See Anna Lee Cundiff.

McBride, Annie Gorman (Wood) (1890 to 1962) – Wife of James Howett McBride, Mother of James Howett McBride (Jr.), Sherwell McBride Timmons, Hal Shearon McBride, Sr. and Anna Lee McBride Cundiff and Paternal Grandmother to the author (Mema Mac).

McBride, Billie Jean (Martin) (1938-) – Wife to Hal S. McBride, Jr., Mother to David Grant McBride and James Michael McBride and “One of those pretty little Martin girls” (Lou Martin Mattox, Annice Martin Reynolds, Pauline Martin Ross, and Billie Martin McBride).

McBride, David Grant (1957-) – Eldest son of Hal S. McBride, Jr. and Billie Jean McBride.

McBride, Follie Belle (Lane) (1918-2003) – Wife to H. Shearon McBride, Sr., Mother to Hal S. McBride, Jr. and James Lane McBride, Youngest daughter of O.B. and Marvella Lane, and served as Haskell County Tag Agent and Secretary of the Haskell County Election Board. (Mother)

McBride, Hal Shearon, Sr. (1916 to 1993) – Husband of Follie Belle Lane McBride, Father to Hal Shearon McBride, Jr. and James Lane McBride, Youngest son of J. H. and Annie McBride, and owner of McBride Radio and Television. (Dad)

McBride, Hal Shearon, Jr. (1937 -) – Husband to Billie Jean Martin McBride, Father to David Grant McBride and James Michael McBride, Eldest son of H. Shearon McBride, Sr. and Follie Belle McBride and author of this memoir.

McBride, James Howett (1888 to 1958) – Husband to Annie Gorman McBride, Father to J. Howett McBride, Sherwell McBride Timmons, Hal Shearon McBride, Sr. and Anna Lee McBride Cundiff, Operator of Hays and Buchanan Dry Goods Company and Paternal Grandfather to the author. (Bepa Mac, Mr. Mac)

McBride, James Lane (1940 to 1987) – Husband to Wilma Lee Sunday McBride, Father to Shari Lynn McBride Malthaner and Sandy Lee McBride Brewer, Youngest son of H. S. and Follie Belle McBride and brother to the author.

McBride, James Michael (1959-) – Youngest son of Hal Shearon McBride, Jr. and Billie Jean McBride.

McBride, J. Howett – Eldest son of James Howett and Annie Gorman McBride, Husband to Ada C. Barnett McBride, Father to Linda Jane McBride Skaer and John Howett McBride, retired as Coordinator of Elementary Schools, Bartlesville, Oklahoma and Uncle to the author.

McBride, Missouri Emily (Shearon) (1862 to 1937) – Wife to

Sherwell Keir McBride, Mother to James H. McBride, Great-grandmother to the author.

McBride, Sherwell Keir (1854-1900?) – Husband to Missouri Emily Shearon, Father to James H. McBride, Great-grandfather to the author.

McBride, Sherwell – See Sherwell Timmons.

McConnell, Woodrow – Boyhood friend of H. Shearon McBride, Sr. and alleged participant in the "ice cream theft".

Riley, Lillian – English teacher at Stigler High School.

Roberts, "Preacher" – Minister and housing contractor in Haskell County, Oklahoma.

Rushing, Leo – Teacher and High School Principal at Stigler High School.

Sigmon, Ally – Wife of Lloyd Sigmon and Sister of Hubert Claunts.

Sigmon, Lloyd – Husband of Ally Claunts Sigmon and Stigler businessman.

Thomas, Illa Hale (1901-1965) – Wife to Lucian B. Thomas, Mother of James William Thomas and Gloria Jean Thomas.

Thomas, James William (Jimmy) (1937-) – Childhood neighbor and lifelong friend of the author.

Thomas, Lucian B. (1893-1970) – Husband to Illa Thomas, Father to James William Thomas and Gloria Jean Thomas, owner of Western Auto Supply Store, Stigler, Oklahoma.

Timmons, Sherwell – Daughter of James H. and Annie Gorman McBride, Wife to Dr. Nolan David Timmons, Father to Kay

Timmons Hames and David Timmons and Aunt to the author.

Timmons, Nolan David – Husband to Sherwell McBride Timmons, Father to Kay Timmons Hames and David Timmons, Dentist in Fort Worth, Texas, and Uncle to the author.

PROLOGUE

This writing had its genesis in the curiosity and with the encouragement of my eldest granddaughter, Emily Ann McBride-Tichenor. I remain somewhat at a loss to explain why I chose to complete it.

Perhaps, as some veteran is said to have observed, "They are only lost when no one remembers them." I feel the need to make an effort to see that at least the essence of those to whom I am so indebted is sustained in the cognitive network of our evolving family; preventing them from completely vanishing into the abyss of obscurity to which we are prone to allow those who comprise our family histories to become assigned.

I sincerely hope that my heirs, most of who are yet to be born, will view this effort a gift.

I was born Hal Shearon McBride, Jr. on February 22, 1937 to Hal Shearon McBride, Sr. and Follie Belle Lane McBride in the rural southern Oklahoma community of Stigler located in an area commonly referred to as "Little Dixie". Oklahoma had not yet been a state 30 years.

Mother's nickname was Jinkie and Daddy's nickname was Poo. I was Jinky Poo until I started school. It seems that at that time my Mother insisted – by accounts very adamantly and relentlessly insisted -- that I was to be called Hal.

My paternal grandparents were James Howett McBride and Anna Woods McBride. My maternal grandparents were Oscar

Breckinridge Lane and Marvella Lane. I called my grandfathers "Beba" and my grandmothers "Mema".

There were four McBride children, James Howett McBride, Sherwell McBride (Timmons), Hal Shearon McBride, Sr. and Anna Lee McBride (Cundiff).

There were five Lane children, Vivian Lane (Claunts), Lacy Lane, Ruth Lane (Lightfoot), Archie Lane, and Follie Belle Lane (McBride).

The most significant single event in my life occurred on November 21, 1956 in Sallisaw, Oklahoma. Billie Jean Martin and I were married.

I was born into the Great Depression, perhaps not at its peak but the Depression certainly was not yet waning. I was almost 5 years old when Pearl Harbor was bombed and my early school years were during World War II.

I grew up in the midst of people who had chosen to stay in rural Oklahoma during the Great Depression. They had labored and sacrificed to hold on to their stores and to their farms, to someway survive --- and survive they did.

They were a stubborn, proud and pragmatic group that weathered the depression and the onslaughts of nature on somewhat their own terms. I know that the character of this determined and optimistic merchant class that at one time dotted the rural southern plains influenced me. This memoir reflects not only the experiences of my parents and grandparents, but most likely in many ways, each with their own individual variations, the story of the families of almost all of my classmates at Stigler High School in the 1950's.

I have become convinced that each of us has many stories to share, stories that include those for whom we cared so very much. I choose to share these stories. These stories are true to my very best recollection. I hope others in my family and others from my hometown town, a town which I so value, will choose to write their recollections.

I think that the Great Depression, rural Oklahoma and World War II, each in its unique way, influenced all of my generation. I believe that it is the people we love and have loved; the personal experiences that we shall carry with us through the always-evolving experience of life; from birth to death that shape us. We are never static, but rather are always being altered by the episodes of our lives and by the people who share themselves with us.

While at times I found it to be quite uncomfortable, the writing of these recollections has been an exceptional learning experience.

PART ONE

BEGINNINGS

ONE

My great grandfather, Sherwell Keir McBride, was born February 13, 1854 in Pennsylvania. He was reared and educated in this region.

After obtaining an undergraduate degree from Lafayette College in Easton, Pennsylvania, he graduated from Rush Medical College, Chicago.

He practiced medicine, following the Scottish-Irish coal miners as they migrated westerly toward new coalfields, as one field was mined out another seemed to open just to the west. Such a migrant lifestyle was likely quite judicious for a physician with an alcohol problem.

At some point, he met and married Missouri Emily Shearon. She was described as a lovely young woman regrettably possessed of an ill-temper. She was a native of Arkansas having been born in 1863 in Conway, Arkansas to William and Eisora Shearon, both of Scottish descent.

There were three children of this union. My grandfather, James Howett McBride, born in 1888, was the middle child. He had two sisters, Tomasina, "Tom" born in 1886 and Sherwell, born in 1891.

I know that my Grandfather was proud of his sisters and that over the years they corresponded with some regularity, but I never met them. Both sisters obtained adequate education to become teachers in Louisiana. One of his two nephews, Carl

Maddox became the athletic director at Louisiana State University and Mississippi State University. The other, Kier Maddox, taught mathematics in the Louisiana university system.

Sherwell Keir and Missouri Emily McBride had made their way to Huntington, Arkansas. It was in Huntington that his alcoholism so impaired him that he was institutionalized, consistent with the treatment of the time. He died in about 1900, a resident of the Arkansas State Lunatic Asylum in Little Rock.

To help support the family whose income was limited to what Missouri Emily earned by taking in two boarders, Granddaddy McBride went to work in the coalmines of Huntington, Arkansas at the age of 12. His first job was caring for the mules in the mines. The mules pulled the rail cars filled with coal from the site of extraction to the surface.

He once told me of his coalmine employment, "I knew a bad deal when I had one, but I kept after it till I could find a better job." And he did. When he was 15 years old, he took a job in a market and dry goods store in Huntington. He was to remain in some form of mercantile; plying what became a special enthusiasm for shoes as best possible, the rest of his life. Through a blend of intelligence, common sense and curiosity he would develop into an extremely innovative marketer of clothing.

I cannot recall the name of the man who first employed him, but I do recall driving Granddaddy to his funeral in Huntington, Arkansas. For my grandfather to take a day away from the store for something other than business or a mysterious illness well-known in our family as "the World Series flu", this had to have been a significant man in his life. It must have been the summer of 1953 because I recall driving the first vehicle my father owned, a 1947 green Chevy pickup.

It was mid-summer and the temperature was sweltering. We had driven to Huntington with the windows open. Granddad sat straight-backed with his Panama straw hat in his lap. We went to his friend's home, Bob Jack, before the services likely for several reasons, but getting his wind blown hair neatly combed was absolutely one of those reasons. So, at his insistence, I drove the truck back up the hill to the church with the windows rolled up. I pulled up near the front of the Church and let him out. He stepped from that old green pickup truck appearing utterly unruffled, hat in hand and every hair in place.

The services where conducted in a stone church on the west side of the highway. I was grateful that the church was filled and there were people standing outside next to the windows to hear the service. This gave me an excuse to walk to a nearby station; purchase a bottle of Coca-Cola along with a package of peanuts to pour into the coke. I then sought shade and conversation under a large tree across the highway from the church where several others of my age had come to escape the funeral and the sun. I discovered that my chunky, fizzing drink of coke and peanuts was not the common practice in Huntington.

TWO

It is only after age has begin to collect it's toll from them; after the lessons of their own lives have sculpted them, that we come to know those adults who will be so significant during our youth. Nonetheless, these are the people who will directly influence our lives and will vicariously have an effect on the lives of all those who come to know us well. It is a complex undertaking to visualize our parents in their youth, much less to seek to obtain a grasp of the youth of our grandparents.

I have contemplated how my Grandfather McBride, James Howett McBride, Sr., might have felt that late summer afternoon in 1921 as he got off the train in Stigler, Oklahoma. I do not know if Stigler was even his intended destination when he boarded the train in Muskogee.

As to his coming to Stigler, he would later joke, "I only had enough money in my pocket to buy a ticket this far." I never believed that, he was a far too deliberate and meticulous man.

The feed and grain business in Muskogee which he had begin with a partner a couple of years earlier had failed in a recession following World War I. He would only say that it was a matter of unfortunate timing and bad decisions.

A small framed, sinewy Irishman, his red hair covered by a panama straw hat, walking along that dusty brick path that led from the railroad station three blocks to Stigler's main intersection in the humidity and heat of an Oklahoma August, strolling into uncertainty.

He stopped in the shade of the last tree of a row of Catalpa trees that lined the walkway from the railroad station into Stigler. He took off his panama straw hat, retrieved a white handkerchief from his right hip pocket, wiping first his forehead then taking the handkerchief and cleaning the leather headband of the straw hat. He retrieved a comb from the same hip pocket and combed his hair with a repetitive precise stroke. He carefully folded the handkerchief back into its original square figure, and then placed both comb and handkerchief back into his pocket. He was an unemployed man preparing to apply for employment.

There he was walking toward the buildings of Stigler, 33 years old and married with 4 children, with no business and without a job. He had left his family in Muskogee until he could remedy that situation.

He would speak of his walk to town and of the mid-day sun reflecting off the Masonic building (Originally the C.S. Stigler Building). I am not certain what he believed he saw, but I know it was despite the fact that he had seen a building suggesting a clear Masonic presence. He never held the Masons in high regard. To the contrary, he was quite suspicious of their motives, questioning the need for such "secret organizations". While this misgiving was in all probability rooted in the Irish experience in America, the Masons and the Klan seemed in some way connected in his mind.

Even if various qualms from the Irish experience at times

intruded upon his logic and his psyche, there was also a sturdy optimism that had taken root from his personal experiences. An intuitive hopefulness that can rise from the confidence one gains from surviving difficulty with dignity.

He expected to find a job and he did.

By nightfall, a Stigler merchant of Jewish descent by the name of Meyer had employed him in a local dry goods store. He came to so respect this man that some 30 years later he would still be quoting the fundamentals of Mr. Meyer's retail philosophy. My grandfather believed with considerable conviction that you could learn something from every person you would encounter in life.

"You must listen well and share little."

This was the advice, maybe more of a directive; that I would receive repeatedly over my youth.

During his lunch hour the next day, his first day on the job at Meyers Dry Goods, he walked back to the train station and telegraphed the news to his wife, Mema Mac. Their eldest child, Howett, would recall how excited she was when the telegram was delivered.

Apparently he had somehow gotten out the Muskogee Feed and Grain failure with an amount of cash. Within a week, he bought the house at 605 N.W. "A" Street and the two adjoining lots to the west. He again wired Mema Mac for her and the kids to come. It seems that he had a steadfast resolve that Stigler was to be the place he would raise his family. They were not to move again.

For all the emotions Annie Gorman Wood McBride, Mema Mac, might have felt unloading four small children in front of the house at 605 N.W. "A" Street, I do not believe that she lacked confidence in her survival skills. Her experiences in her native Kilmarnock, Scotland and during her immigration to the United States in 1906 always seemed to me to have imbued her with self-assurance about her capacity to meet a challenge.

At 16 years of age, she had made the Atlantic crossing alone completing the journey by train to Alton, Illinois where her brother, Jimmy Wood, was working in the coalfields.

Two years after her arrival in this country, she made a trip to Huntington, Arkansas to spend the summer with two cousins whose husbands had left Alton for jobs in coal fields of Huntington. So the story goes she began to favor a certain general store because of a young clerk who worked there. She married that clerk, my grandfather, and she never returned to Alton.

They were to have 4 children, James Howett McBride, Sherwell McBride Timmons, Hal Shearon McBride (Sr.) and Anna Lee McBride Cundiff.

Just as Roy "Dad" Bankhead would become Granddaddy's closest friend in Stigler, Bob Jack, who like my grandfather had fled the mines to farming, was his close, life long Huntington friend.

While I know Bob Jack loved his land, I believe that he loved his whiskey still more. And it was that still that made his farming life a profitable enterprise.

The common element to the birth of a McBride child in Huntington was that Granddaddy would sit on the curb across the street from the house with Bob Jack, sipping the whiskey from Bob's personal stock, and await the child's arrival. The eldest, Howett, remembered getting to sit with them when the youngest, Anna Lee, was born and how much like grown up it made him feel.

Such behavior would have been very inconsistent for the man I knew in my youth, but when it was mentioned it always brought a wry smile that covered my grandfather's face.

So, at the age of 3, my father, Shearon McBride, arrived in Stigler along with his mother, his older brother, James Howett, Jr., his older sister, Sherwell, and the toddler, Anna Lee. As their father seemed to intend, they were to grow up in Stigler.

Mema Mac was a broad shouldered woman with the Scottish set of jaw and that Scottish chin. She would successfully rear their children during some trying times, adolescents during the Great Depression. Those times could have only served to enhance her feelings of confidence in her ability to survive; in her independence. Such personal convictions can also be isolating, she had no friends beyond her family.

And over the years, it was Granddaddy who reinforced her feelings of uniqueness. He spoiled her rotten and she was there for the spoiling. She loved it and she loved him.

As with virtually every wife of her time who had a telephone, she would call her daily order into a grocery store or a market. The order would then be delivered on either a morning or an afternoon delivery route; Granddaddy paid a premium to have her grocery order delivered within an hour of her call.

Beyond that, the Dr. Pepper deliveryman would bring her cases to her back door. It impressed me if not her neighbors and she certainly took great pleasure in having that delivery truck come to her home. The sure indicator of an imminent visit from my cousins would be the appearance of a case of orange and a case of strawberry pop beside her Dr. Pepper. I don't know if my cousins actually enjoyed the flavored soda, but she loved purchasing it for them.

Friday was her day at the beauty shop. She would walk the few blocks to the beauty shop to have her hair done. It was an every Friday, rain or shine, ritual.

It is possible that this very special treatment was connected to her relationship with Missouri Emily McBride, Granddaddy's mother, who would quickly come to live about a block to the west of my Grandparents in Stigler. I know little of her. She died in 1938 so I know only two things.

It seems that she and Mema Mac were "water and oil". And in concurring with Mema Mac's harsh descriptions of her, Howett and Daddy found a rare area of total agreement. They agreed that she was one very difficult and demanding woman who was very resentful of "that Scottish immigrant girl who married her son". An interesting cognitive inconsistency since I believe that both of her parents were Scottish immigrants.

THREE

Of my mother's family, the first to arrive in Stigler was her eldest sister, Vivian Lane Claunts. Vivian and her husband, Hubert Claunts located in Stigler in 1926, opening the Stigler 5 and Up on Halloween of 1926.

Over the passage of time, my Mother, Follie Belle Lane, and my Grandmother Lane, Marvella Hammock Lane, would follow, by their own diverse paths to make their homes in Stigler.

With that said, it was a family death the predicated both their relocations to Stigler to live with Vivian and Hubert Claunts. My mother, Follie Belle Lane, came in 1934 to live with her sister and brother-in-law after the death of her oldest brother, Lacy, in Oklahoma City.

I know that Mema Lane arrived in Stigler in 1939, following the death of her husband, O.B. Lane, near Brentwood, Arkansas, to live with her eldest daughter and her husband, Vivian and Hubert Claunts.

Marvella Hammock met and married Oscar Breckinridge Lane in Fort Smith, Arkansas. At the time, he was a night watchman at a furniture factory who wrote poetry to pass the quiet of the night.

I never really got to know him. He died in 1938. The only tale I would regularly hear was about how disappointed he was that I wouldn't ride a goat he had in the mountains.

They had five children. The eldest was Vivian Pearl Lane

(Claunts). It was Vivian's girlhood escapades resulting in her marriage to Hubert Claunts that would eventually lead to my Mother and Mema Lane coming to Stigler.

Ruth Velma Lane (Nicodemus) (Grace) (Lightfoot), Lacy Leo Lane, Archie James Lane, and my mother, Follie Belle Lane (McBride) followed in age. All their children were born in Fort Smith, Arkansas.

To regress, Mema Lane was born Marvella Hammock. She spent the first months of her life in St. Joseph, Missouri. It was very difficult to get her to speak of her parents. It was embedded in family lore that her mother and her father were Mormon and they were involved in a religiously inspired quarrel that resulted in their moving to Ft. Smith, Arkansas.

While she would make up stories of her childhood, she would never really speak of her family. Over the years, she attended several churches in Stigler, but never the First Baptist Church that her eldest child, Vivian, so relished. She did have until her death a Book of Mormon as a companion to her well-worn Bible. But like the snuff she dipped, it was generally kept concealed.

Mema Lane would hint at perhaps a less likely but more nefarious and intriguing story. It is true that she was born in February of 1882 in St. Joseph, Missouri. In April of 1882 in St. Joseph, Jesse James was shot and killed. While Mema Lane told the story of the event, I did on one occasion hear her older sister talk of living across the street from the James' house and of playing in the James' home just prior to his being shot. Her parents did promptly leave St. Joseph and relocated in Fort Smith.

There was always this subtle hint that her father was somehow affiliated with the James family and continued to conduct some less than legal activities in Indian Territory. When ask about her father's vocation, her standard response was, "He worked". She did say he traveled a lot in his work and that he would be home for sizeable periods of time with a propensity to spend almost all of his time inside the home during the daylight hours and having to keep the windows covered when he was home. It seems that even my mother knew very little of her Grandfather Hammock. *(Jack Lane, Lacy's son, nor Boots Claunts, Vivian's eldest son, knew anything of him and could not recall ever hearing of his line of work.)*

The snuff, her "true crime" magazines, the Grit Newspaper (a weekly newspaper that arrived by mail and was widely popular with farm families) and a glass of wine in the quiet before bedtime, those were the luxuries of Mema Lane's life. And you should never mistake the importance these simple things had to this plainspoken and frank woman.

Christianity was very vital to her existence, but she would share her beliefs and her knowledge only if ask. While she enjoyed the community of a church, she would be very clear that there were Sunday mornings on her front porch in the Ozark Mountains that were as spiritual as any moments in her life.

Intellectually, Mema Lane was a sturdy and direct individual rarely leaving a person guessing about her feelings or opinions. Once in the nursing home a likely well intended but religiously enthusiastic employee decided that Mema did not need her evening wine. By dark on the next evening, Dr. Thomas (Conklin) had written her a "prescription" for 8 ounces of bedtime wine with 8 more ounces upon her request.

On another occasion, Billie and I had not been to Stigler to see her for a while; Mother had been making excuses for us by telling her how busy we were. We received a simple note stating, "If you are too busy to come see me, you are too damn busy."

We drove to Stigler the next Saturday.

As is the sequence of life, I really only came to know her after she had buried both of her sons, Archie who died at 3, Lacy who died at 30, and her husband, her beloved Oscar, who died in 1938. In her 90's, in the Stigler Nursing Home, she would say the most difficult thing about living to her age or for that matter in life was burying your children. While she would speak ever so fondly of Lacy, it seemed to be Archie that she grieved so deeply. Archie's death at 3, in 1911, was something that Mema Lane would never discuss in depth. She would only say that he died of "the fever." I came to understand that despite all logic to the contrary, she somehow believed that there should have been something that she could have done that would have saved him.

FOUR

Back to the progression toward Stigler, it seems that at 14, Aunt Vivian literally left home to travel with a carnival that was passing through Fort Smith. Granddaddy Lane saw it as a waste of his good time and effort to pursue his willful and impulsive eldest daughter.

The carnival weaved its way through the communities of western Arkansas and eastern Oklahoma, ultimately paying a visit to Warner, Oklahoma in the fall of 1917, possibly associated with some local celebration. It was there that a promising young merchant, the son of a prominent Whitefield family, Hubert Claunts, spotted the 15 year-old Vivian Lane. By all accounts, she was beautiful and filled with a spectacular energy.

Hubert Claunts was born into a well-established family in Whitefield, which was considered to be the most flourishing community in Haskell County as the 19th Century came to a close. His father, John Wesley Claunts, was the first teacher at the Whitefield Academy founded in 1884. There was a school founded before the Civil War and resumed shortly after the Civil War had ended. I am uncertain as to the circumstances that brought the Academy into existence.

They married on February 10, 1918. Hubert would later tell all who would listen, "I found my love in a 5 and dime." Should Mema Lane be within earshot, she would snort, "A traveling 5 and dime!"

Their two sons, Hubert Bluford "Boots" Claunts, born March 21, 1919, and John W. "Tag" Claunts (born Rupert Wesley Claunts), born in February of 1920, arrived in Warner. The nickname "Boots" came from Tag's attempts to pronounce and mispronounce Bluford, Boots middle name. "Tag" being the younger, was a tag-a-long.

It is my understanding that they later had two daughters, both of whom died either at birth or in infancy. Aunt Vivian never spoke of them that I heard. I have searched for the graves in the cemetery in Warner, Oklahoma, but have never been able to identify them.

I understand the Warner store thrived until some economic downturn in the 1920's. And then its demise was rapid. Vivian and Hubert relocated and opened the Stigler 5 and Up. It is likely that there were two major factors involved. One, two wholesalers in Fort Smith were very encouraging to Hubert to establish another store.

While I was in high school, I drove Uncle Hubert to Fort Smith to buy at Beall's to whom he remained quite loyal and to another wholesaler. Afterward we would eat at Constantio's, a long time Barbeque restaurant on the east side of Garrison Avenue not far from the river. It still had a mahogany bar that ran the length of building on the south side and booths with incredibly high dividing walls between the booths – they seemed to reach to the ceiling. The beans were still placed in individual pots and then baked in brick ovens located behind the restaurant and the ribs – ah, the ribs. Billie and I ate there on occasion when we were dating.

Second, I am convinced that Stigler was selected because Hubert's older sister, Ally, had married Lloyd Sigmon, one of the Sigmon brothers who were pioneer eastern Oklahoma merchants and for whom Hubert had worked at an earlier time. Lloyd Sigmon had invested in property and owned a significant amount of Stigler along with the cash resources to continue acquiring property during the depression. Ally wanted her younger brother in Stigler, so a storefront near the Sigmon Hotel became available. Vivian and Hubert came to Stigler with Boots and Tag in tow.

The Stigler 5 and Up emerged. I cannot imagine the Stigler of my youth without the Stigler 5 & Up.

FIVE

As with many families, the depression had sent Granddaddy and Mema Lane moving. His job as a night watchman at a Fort Smith furniture factory had "played out". By that time my mother was the only child left in the home. Granddaddy Lane acquired a farm at Low Gap, near Brentwood, Arkansas. It was a rocky Ozark mountain farm with a house much of which he constructed himself – with a floor of compacted dirt. I was never led to believe that the night watchman poet was a great farmer, but I would hear of goats and chickens. As with many, they seemed to be surviving and they owned the land.

Then, quite unexpectedly, Mema Lane lost her Oscar. After purchasing a few groceries from the general store in Low Gap, they were walking home. He became short of breath, sat down upon a large rock to rest a bit before resuming their walk home. He went directly to bed when they arrived home at dusky dark and never awakened.

While I heard many stories from others, Mema Lane only spoke to me of his death once and that was while Vivian lay in their home, dying of bone cancer. She spoke of the emotion she felt, such a great sense of loss. "The last man in my life. You get so busy just trying to live – I don't know if he ever knew --" I still remember wanting to her finish that statement. After that afternoon I had no question about how much she had cared for him and how much she missed him over those years. She always referred to him as "My Oscar" and to her death went by Mrs. O.B. Lane.

Following Granddaddy Oscar's death, Mema Lane came to Stigler to live with her eldest daughter, Vivian and her husband, Hubert Claunts. She took care of the cooking, the cleaning and the laundry while they worked at their Five and Dime. She would bake daily, often baking two different kinds of pies so that Vivian's boys, Boots and Tag, and Hubert could each have a pie that they liked.

And I can never erase nor do I want to, the memory of the smell of her potato rolls baking in the oven.

Nonetheless, for the rest of her life, Mema Lane was regularly drawn back to the mountains and to the cemetery at Brentwood, Arkansas.

Often on Summer Sundays, Vivian and Hubert would drive her there. Aunt Vivian especially enjoyed the fried chicken at the Mountainaire Restaurant on Mount Gaylor.

I enjoyed the metal tower there that gave you a view of Ozarks. As I recall, for a nickel you could climb the tower. I considered it great fun to move up the tower at a pace faster than any adult who had the misfortune to be assigned to accompany me on the climb could match. I find the memory of summer breezes at the top of that metal tower to be irresistible. I don't know why Vivian and Hubert would seemingly always take me on those Sunday outings, but I am thankful they did.

In all the visualizations I have of my grandmothers, both are always in aprons. Yet, I can find no photographs of them wearing an apron. Mema Lane a half-apron of her own making. Mema Mac a full apron with ruffles surrounding the openings for her arms.

Mema Lane baked, but it was Mema Mac knew a thousand and one ways to cook potatoes. For Mema Mac, potatoes were a staple of every meal – every meal. And on potato patty night, surrounded by fresh vegetables, they were the centerpieces of the meal.

Potatoes were grown in and dug from their garden and storied under the house on sheets of corrugated metal. I would be sent to crawl under the house, flashlight in hand and mind filled with visions of spiders and other various creepy, crawly creatures, to retrieve the potatoes.

There was her toast rescued from the gas broiler after it had burnt black around the edges, after scraping the edges with a kitchen knife, she would declared it to be “just good and brown”.

But of all the food, it was Mema Mac’s shortbread that I coveted.

SIX

Before the fall of 1934, Granddaddy Lane decided that his baby daughter Follie Belle, my mother, needed to continue her education beyond the 8 years offered in Low Gap. So, Mother was sent to Oklahoma City to live with her older brother, Lacy and his family. (Jack Lane, Lacy Lane's son, would have been a first grader or so.) She attended Oklahoma City Central High School.

Mema Lane, in her later years, enjoyed spreading the story that Follie Belle had taken far too great an interest in a young man who owned a splendid horse. This infatuation had brought great consternation to her father. And this was the real reason for sending her to Oklahoma City.

As the result of an ill-fated incident, Lacy died of rabies. At his doorstep, he reached down to pet a small dog that had followed him home. The dog bit him and sprinted away. The death that ensued must have been incredibly painful. An indelible impression was left upon my Mother. James received two different sets of rabies shots following squirrel bites. News of a rabid dog sighting in town would keep James and I confined to the house or back yard for days.

Following Lacy's death, Mother came to Stigler to live with Vivian and Hubert. She was to go to school and help with the 5 and dime.

The story goes that when Follie Belle Lane and Shearon

McBride first laid eyes on each other, in the Stigler 5 and Up, it was love at first sight. This is one of the few stories that seemed to be consistent through out the family, from teller to teller.

Daddy apparently had something of a reputation as "unruly and rowdy", prone to practical jokes and to drink a little too much at times. Vivian disapproved of him. She had another type of young man in mind for her baby sister whom she considered to be the brightest of the family. My Aunt Vivian was less than enthusiastic about Follie Belle's infatuation. To make matters worse, Daddy was reported to have been completely smitten.

In his early teens, Dad was displaying enough boisterous behavior that Granddaddy found it troubling.

I know that Anna Lee never forgave Daddy for the "Great Ice Cream Theft". It seems that there was a summer lawn party complete with the hanging lanterns, music, and the girls in their finest dresses, Stigler's version of a Jay Gatsby affair. Daddy and a friend of his, Woodrow McConnell, who were not invited to the function, slipped through a hedge and made off with a freezer of ice cream that had been cranked and covered to firm it. They took it to another hedgerow about a block away, ate their fill and returned the half-eaten container neatly to its original position. What the people who opened the freezer saw was a compromised ice cream container with two spoons sticking in the middle. Anna Lee swears she knew immediately it was the handy work of Woodrow and Shearon.

Whatever the exact cause, Dad was sent for a summer with

Bob Jack and his wife, Johnnie, on their farm that sat at the base of a hill just south of Huntington. Granddaddy felt that a summer in the fields might provide his youngest son with a much needed change in prospective.

Bob's existence was certainly basic. His life was farming, distilling and fermenting. He was dedicated to consuming the fruits of his labors.

Even when I was a teenager, Bob Jack had a significant amount of land under cultivation. I know that it was only when Johnnie threatened to leave him; sometime in the early 1950's that he finally had a bath and toilet installed in the house. It seems that he stubbornly clung to the belief that certain bodily functions were just not intended to occur inside the home, so he continued to use his outdoor toilet.

My Dad only remembered helping "Uncle Bob" harvest his grapes, blackberries and strawberries from the hillside to make wine, a venture he had added to his production endeavors. He also learned how to operate the still that it appears Bob felt compelled to sustain, something of a civic obligation. I know that during that summer, my father developed an affection for Bob and Johnnie Jack that was to continue throughout his life.

Vivian and Hubert hired someone to drive my Mother to Brentwood on Christmas Eve of 1935, after finishing the Christmas rush at the Stigler 5 & Up, to spend the rest of the holiday with her parents.

After Christmas Day of 1935, Daddy took the bus to

Brentwood. He would recall that the one-way ticket cost 60 cents. He would always say that it was best money he ever spent. There was no bus station at Low Gap or Brentwood, so you would pull on a cord that ran the length of the bus as you were approaching the location that you wanted to get off.

Mother was waiting for him at the general store. On horseback, they rode the two miles back into the mountains to the house that Granddaddy Lane had built. It now had a fireplace built of native stone, but the floor remained compacted dirt.

The work bench Granddaddy Lane used in the construction of that cabin is now in our living room.

Mema Lane would speak of being suspicious but would concede, "Oscar and your Daddy did seem to get on well".

On the morning of December 29, 1935, Mother and Dad walked the two mile lane that led to general store. They stood beside the road, much like our city bus stops of today, waiting for the bus. They took the bus to Greenwood, Arkansas, a location they felt was safe from discovery, and were married. Although Boots claims he and Tag figured it out, Vivian wasn't told until after both had graduated from Stigler High School in the Class of 1936.

As had been suspected, Vivian did not approve. But then Aunt Vivian disapproved of everyone who married one of her sisters and most certainly one of her sons.

It was only with this writing that I have become aware that there was always a considerable distance between my McBride grandparents and Aunt Vivian and Uncle Hubert. Mema Lane would occasionally ask me, “How is Mrs. Mac?” Of course I am completely certain that Aunt Vivian, with her ardent commitment to the Southern Baptist philosophy, found my Grandfather McBride’s unmistakably agnostic viewpoints distressing.

I know that he held organized religion in some distain, but he always “held his tongue”. And Mema Lane would refer her eldest daughter’s religious predilection as “uppity”.

SEVEN

Not long before her death, I ask my Mother when she had realized that Daddy was the love of her life. While the question was asked in a rather off-handed manner, there was nothing casual about the reply I received. As she lay in that nursing home bed it was as if the moment had occurred only yesterday.

When she began, I expected an answer that would predate their marriage. But she began to tell me of a May afternoon in 1936 shortly after their high school graduation. She recounted sitting on a quilt in the shade of a tree by a field of yellow flowers on a small hill overlooking the Blue Hole of Mountain Fork Creek to the south of Stigler. The warmth and softness of a southern breeze as it stirred the yellow wild flowers seemed fixed in her memory. She was so proud of the picnic basket packed with fried chicken that she had prepared and which sat on the quilt next to her. She could still describe with incredible detail the rhythmic movement of my father, shirtless, waist deep in the flowing stream and meticulously fly fishing the Blue Hole.

Done with his fishing, he came sloshing up the hillside, pants soaking wet despite the waders, with a moderately dry shirt slung over his shoulder and carrying a stringer of fish. She made him sound like a proud masculine calamity. She laughed at the telling. She said, "That's when I knew." Adding, "Your daddy always liked my fried chicken."

After high school, Daddy took a full time job in Frix

Grocery. He stocked and delivered groceries, aspiring to become a butcher at that point in his life. After living with Mema Mac and Granddaddy until after I was born, we moved into a rent house on Main Street, State Hiway 9 in the spring of 1937.

I know that this house was one door removed from Jimmy Thomas' home. He was born on February 21, 1937, the day before I was. I have no recollection of school years in Stigler that do not include him.

I do remember some things of living in that house. Milk was delivered by a local dairyman. You would indicate the amount of ice you wanted for the ice box by setting the dial on a sign in the window to the desired weight. I thought that the ice tongs used to bring the ice in the back door were ingenious devices.

It was in this house that I was given my first real pet and I remember it most vividly. It was unique. In the very early spring of 1942, it arrived by post in a small box, maybe 1x1x6, with holes in the side from Dad's baby sister, Ann and her husband, Elic Cundiff. For whatever military reason, Elic was based at Fort Benning, Georgia and they sent me something in a box that moved around and hissed.

Not knowing its contents, Mother had set the box on the porch railing of the house until Daddy came home. Daddy and I opened the box. It was a baby alligator.

An alligator through the mail in a box! In retrospect, I know Mother was at least somewhat relieved that Elic who enjoyed a prank as much as Daddy hadn't sent a snake.

I remember I was really excited. I recall some angst about being able to keep my alligator; it was a "wait until your daddy gets home" circumstance. But when Daddy came home from work the next day, he brought some heavy small mesh screen wire. I had a sand box on the east side of the house built of 2x6's, one sturdy sand box.

We half buried a well-worn enamel dishpan in one corner which could be easily filled with water, then nailed the screen mesh over the sand box leaving just enough of an opening that I could raise that corner and feed the very small alligator.

I went to Aunt Vivian and Uncle Hubert's home, which housed the only set of encyclopedias I knew of and Mema Lane read to me about alligators. Mema Mac helped me find Okefenokee Swamp in Georgia where Ann and Elic purchased the alligator.

If I named that alligator, I don't remember the name. But I likely did as I was prone to name every animal with which I came into contact.

Given the nourishing scraps that Daddy brought home from Frix butcher shop, my alligator flourished. I thought that when he hissed at me as I raised the wire at the corner of his pen that he was being friendly, rather like a cat purring. Gratefully, I never had to discover otherwise. The truth is I was proud of my alligator. Needless to say, it was unique; none of my friends had such pets. My friends really seemed to enjoy watching me feed him in the late afternoons, even those who kept their distance and did not view him the same affection I did.

He grew rapidly. By early fall, he dug his way out along the moist base of the box by the dishpan. He made his way about a block before he was run over and killed in the driveway of Skinny McDaniel's filling station (NE corner of 2nd and Main).

I buried him next to his sand box at the base of the house.

I don't know what those who saw him thought of an alligator waddling it's way across that service station and what on earth the traveler's who ran over him believed. I do know that while James was in high school, he worked for Clennie Stevens who witnessed the demise of my alligator. Clennie still talked about it.

Even today, I savor the idea that some years from now an anthropologist or archeologist might some day excavate the foundation of that house and ponder the possibility of an alligator population in Oklahoma. And have the skeleton of an alligator to support that hypothesis.

It was in this house on Main Street that I came down with the mumps and seemingly at the same time the measles. The windows to my bedroom were covered because blindness was said to be a side effect of the measles, but the risk could be prevented if the patient was kept confined to a dark room. I only know that it was scary.

But it was this illness that resulted in a stuffed doll being brought to me that resembled one of the Seven Dwarfs was brought from the Stigler 5 and Up. Floppy arrived and remains in my possession although he is much the worse for the wear and tear.

I recall the clamor about Pearl Harbor and the beginning of the war. I can recall sitting in someone's lap as everyone was huddled around a radio at Granddaddy McBride house. It was somber.

EIGHT

I have no memories of our move to Tulsa when Dad got the job at Douglas Aircraft in the late fall of 1942. But I do remember Tulsa. We lived in Tulsa in a small green frame home on the southwest corner of 12th and Erie.

There was an ice cream and milk store at 11th and Erie, a block from where we lived and on Route 66. I couldn't have an ice cream each day, but it seems I went to that store daily nonetheless. I loved watching the activity, sitting on the window sill outside the store I could watch the people moving in and out of the store and the traffic moving along 66.

There was a Safeway that I thought was incredible in the building at 11th and Yale near where Talley's Café is now located. It seemed so large compared to Frix's Store in Stigler. But unlike Frix's, Mother would never send me there alone to secure bread or other small items.

I was in the first grade at Franklin Elementary School. I liked it and I believe my Mother liked it. I surely remember her as being happy in Tulsa. Maybe that led to her painting the house in Stigler green some years later.

It was that Thanksgiving that World War II touched my family in a very personal manner. Anna Lee and her children were staying in Stigler with Grandmother and Granddaddy while Elic Cundiff was overseas. Auntie Ann had driven them all to

Tulsa and Mother had prepared Thanksgiving dinner. No, Mother had labored and fretted over that Holiday dinner.

Thanksgiving morning, while they were in route to Tulsa, a telegram arrived at the Palace Drug in Stigler saying that Elic was missing in action. Small communities being what they were, the Western Union man knew were the family was and forwarded the telegram. The telegram was delivered in Tulsa just before noon. I was confused, but I remember the tears. No one could comfort Anna Lee. Odd, but I recall I felt that it was unfair that it had ruined the dinner at which Mother had worked so hard.

It was several weeks before the news came that Elic had been captured and was in German POW camp somewhere in Italy.

I am uncertain as to the factors that led to Daddy deciding to enlist in the Army in the early spring of 1944, but he did. He had a good paying job with Douglas Aircraft, the reason we had moved to Tulsa, that would have been considered vital to the war effort and he had a family. As I understand it, he would have been exempt from the draft.

I found out about the impending changes in our lives after a man came to the school and watched some softball games during recess. The principal and the man spoke with me about playing baseball during the spring and summer. Such attention pleases young boys. When the man went to talk to my parents, he was told of their plans. It was at that point they told me. I was disappointed.

NINE

World War II inflicted numerous losses in many families and in quite diverse ways. For my father and me, it was a profound and lasting disruption in our relationship. I do believe that he made some efforts during the early years to reach out to me, but we were never really able to reconnect. At 6, I felt he was choosing to leave us and I was angry.

I regret that this always concerned mother and I know from our conversations she always felt that I was responsible for the breech. And perhaps I was.

Daddy moved us back to Stigler and into two rooms of a home a few blocks south of Boone School (the Stigler Elementary School). Then, he left. Mother hung a blue star in the window.

We had only lived there a brief period of time and the older lady who owned the house asked us to leave. The noise of "the children" bothered her.

The front porch wrapped around the south and east sides of the house and the lady who owned the house would sit looking out her window across the south porch and watch the vehicles on State Hiway 9. I vividly remember stomping around the porch until I was certain I had her attention, I turned and looked at her, and then I stuck my tongue out at her.

The lady was startled and appalled. Mother was not pleased. I was okay with it.

I was an angry boy. I am certain that poor Ms. ("Oyama") Williams, my teacher for the few remaining weeks of first grade, had to be so glad to get rid of me. I know that there was discussion about my being promoted to the second grade.

It seems that my school performance and my tongue had caught my Grandfather's attention. This became one of those times, which were few, where Granddaddy McBride stepped in and put his foot down. You did not forget those times.

I was summoned to the store, to his office. His words were direct, expressing possibly the first clear sentiment I remember from anyone.

He said, "I will not tolerate you failing just because you're mad and won't try. You will try." "Be mad, but keep your tongue in your mouth."

I believe he expected tears but none came. He stuck his hand out and I shook it. He had offered no carrot for good conduct, but there was security in knowing that he cared enough to call me to account. And I left his office with a clear understanding of accountability. My grandfather was a precise man. .

I don't believe that he had any desire to become the primary male in my life, having already reared his two sons. With Daddy absent and no one knew for how long, I likely drafted him into parental duty on the home front. And he served and I adored him for his service.

Although I was born in the middle bedroom my Grandfather's home and logic tells me that he was there all of my early life, I have no recollection of him before that day. Although he died over 50 years ago, I don't recall a time since the day we met in his office that I have felt I was without him.

Once again, we moved in with Grandmother and Granddaddy for a time.

My Grandmother McBride, Mema Mac, approached me in a quite different manner. She produced a wicker basket of filled with marbles. The painted wooden floor in the parlor sloped into one corner allowing the marbles to always roll to that area. She turned me loose and I can not even imagine the noise I made smashing those marbles into each other with all the force my thumb could muster. After a therapeutic session in the marble corner I always felt better. And a Dr. Pepper.

It seems that the first day school was out, I was told to watch the large ash tree that sat on the lot line to the west. I likely had little else to do. About mid-morning a dump truck arrived and unloaded a bed full of sand. I don't know how large that sand pile actually was, but I thought it was Mount Everest. After that, until James had outgrown "sand pile", a dump truck filled with sand would arrive at the close of school each year. I don't believe anything can spur a child's imagination like a pile of sand.

Then, we moved to a rent house located at the northeast corner of 5th and Main. Jimmy Thomas was living on the east end of that block. Jimmy and I became frequent visitors to that sand pile.

Alas, by the time my grandchildren arrived, "cat cleanliness syndrome" had made such large open sand piles a parental concern – so, despite repeated efforts, I was barred from providing such a sand pile. Oh, but I was often tempted!

It was during this time that Granddaddy and I begin a ritual of listening to the Friday night fights sponsored by the Gillette Razor Company on the radio. There was popcorn popped on the stove in a skillet with loads of butter and Dr. Peppers all around the room.

My boyhood sports heroes became boxers and baseball players – St. Louis Cardinal Baseball players. I relished tales of the "Gashouse Gang", of Dizzy and Paul Dean and the "Wild Horse of the Osage", Pepper Martin; accounts of current players like Marty Marion and Stan Musial.

Boxing conversation always came to include the much anticipated rematch between Billy Conn and Joe Louis. To the man on the street in Stigler, Billy Conn was winning the pre-war fight until he got careless allowing Joe Louis to knock him out; he would win the rematch. For all the banter of skill and technique, the underlying desire was for the heavyweight champion of the world to once again be a white man. It was racism, accepted and no reason to disguise it.

TEN

Arrangements were made for me to be assigned to the second grade class of Opal Calhoun. Ms. Calhoun was the aunt of Phil and Jon Conard who lived across the street from Granddaddy and Grandmother. It seems her reputation for educational excellence was already established.

My second grade experience was a true stroke of good fortune. Ms. Calhoun moved me in a single year from an angry apathy to an active curiosity, to being a good student and as voracious reader as any second grader can become. For years afterward, her first question to me would be, "What are you reading?" followed by "Please tell me about it". I felt that she really wanted to hear and I was always prepared.

Even as late as my senior year in high school, on a day when the elementary school students had walked to the high school for high school play, she said, "Walk back with me." I can still remember her waving to Leo Rushing, the high school principal, and pointing to me. As an orderly row of second graders preceded Miss Opal and me during the 8-block walk, we discussed Jack London's Sea Wolf. While I recall little of the book now, I know that I left that walk, that conversation, in search of more information about some guy named "Neiche".

From the second grade on, school was wonderful although the topics I might be pursing at given points in time did not always correspond with my teacher's goals. On the whole, I believe that my teachers were much better at teaching than I was at "studenting", but I learned incredible amounts of information.

ELEVEN

During that summer of 1945, Mema Mac took me to visit Aunt Sherwell and Uncle Nolan (Timmons). They were living in Lincoln, Nebraska were the Navy had sent Uncle Nolan to attend dental school. I was thrilled more because Nolan was my favorite childhood Uncle than I was about the trip itself.

As I understand it, it was a miracle that Nolan married Aunt Sherwell because of the manner in which I terrorized him during their courtship. A favorite family story of which I have no recollection involved the creation of a family train – lining up all the available chairs in Mema and Bepa's sitting room and seating the available "passengers" on my train. I, of course, was the engineer. So the story goes, I would vigorously scold anyone who attempted to make a departure while the train was still moving. It seems that my preferred target was Nolan. But then he was such a patient man.

I do recall while they were dating, he had a Ford coupe – for whatever reason I remember it as being a deep maroon. It had the earliest form of in-car climate control – a rubber-bladed fan mounted upon the dash. To the consternation of many, he taught me how to stop the fan blade with my finger – a skill I was to assimilate to every fan. I was so taken by the power of being able to stop the fan blades that despite repeated warnings, I stopped every fan in my reach. As a result I was often sent to the willow tree in the back yard to choose and cut a switch to be used on my legs --- and God forbid the selected limb not be large enough!!!! While writing this, it occurs to me that just maybe "Patient Uncle Nolan" found a way to – but Nolan would never do that.

While I have no recollection as to how Mema and I got to Muskogee, I know we stopped at the Butcher shop Nolan's parents owned and operated. It was just west of the viaduct that traversed the railroad tracks in downtown Muskogee. It seems we picked up some packages for Sherwell and Nolan.

We boarded the train in Muskogee from an open-air platform surfaced with paving bricks. I remember how jam-packed with soldiers the trains were. We had what had been described to me as a long lay-over in Kansas City, but I was so taken by the station. It seems that there were these beautiful ornate arches in a cavernous central area of the station. Interestingly, I remember thinking they seemed to be almost prayerfully reaching skyward. It was one of the few accounts of an experience that seemed to give my Aunt Vivian hope for my ultimate redemption.

Aunt Sherwell and Uncle Nolan were living in a one-bedroom apartment with a shared bathroom. Not unusual for the time, the apartment had been created by the partitioning of a large old house. And there was a rollaway bed rented for the occasion of our visit. And the laundry was in the basement. I didn't think we had basements in Stigler. It seemed to be such an intriguing place, the unfamiliar damp smell and the dim light offered a perfect blend for scary and adventurous flights of imagination.

Nolan was in dental school and Sherwell was working in downtown Lincoln for a 5 and dime, either Kress or Woolworth. Kress and Woolworth's were to me such magical places and I was so impressed with Auntie working behind the glass display case. One day Mema and I rode the bus downtown to the store, had lunch at the lunch counter where I was allowed the luxury of a malt with lunch.

When Nolan came home it was play time. He let me "jump" on the rollaway bed, a forbidden practice in Stigler. Mema scolded us, and then gave in. He took me, over the objections of Mema and Sherwell, to the top of the Capitol building in Lincoln. He encouraged me to see the cars as ants – then, the buildings as made with Erector Sets.

As the play calmed toward bedtime, Uncle Nolan and I would exchange bedtime stories. I loved to make up tall tales of narrow escapes from the terrible creatures that lurked in the basement. He acted as if he was fascinated by them.

To this day I do not know how he did it two weeks, but I left Lincoln knowing Nolan's mantras, "just imagine and just suppose." A fertile and creative imagination was acceptable.

TWELVE

As with all of my generation, I have various memories of World War II. Mostly, it is of the ration stamps for everything from sugar to shoes to gasoline. And each week at school we bought "war bond" stamps to place in book. Every nickel would bring the war closer to an end.

We went to church dressed in our soldier suits.

I know I understood to some degree the gravity of the war; it was all around you and seemingly affected every element of daily life. And in the Stigler of my childhood a Gold Star home was passed quietly and respectfully.

But I was a child, and it didn't seem fair that I couldn't have a bicycle. There were a few bikes sold with Victory tires which had solid synthetic rubber tires requiring no inflation. The ride reflected the solidity. Granddaddy was not to buy me a bicycle until after the war; it was a bicycle with balloon tires constructed of real rubber.

There was an evening practice of sitting together listening to the war news. H.V. Kaltenborn – I suspect few knew his full name was Hans von Kaltenborn – there was sensitivity to German names at the time. But I remember his deep, clear, crisp voice – a direct and to the point manner of delivery. He seemed a serious man for serious times. I know my grandfather found him credible right up to the night he proclaimed Dewey had defeated Truman and Granddaddy went to bed concerned about a

Republican President.

We followed the War by the maps on the front page of the paper. I remember Iwo Jima, D-Day, the Battle of the Bulge, the firestorms over Dresden and the atomic bombs. Iwo Jima was in the headlines of the newspaper and Charlie Stevenson (his dad had the Coca-Cola Bottling Plant in Stigler) and I used a round rag rug as the island, make Mount Sirabaci and used our metal toy battleships to simulate the invasion.

Much of our boyhood play involved soldiers or cowboys. No one would be the enemy, so we were a collection of "good guys".

In retrospect, the only time I can recall thinking that we might be poor – and the thought passed quickly – involved a toy pistol that Vivian and Hubert gave me from the 5 and dime. This pistol has a glorious white handle and a real leather scabbard. Fortunately for me the barrel of the pistol had been broken completely off and was not in the box when it arrived at the store. So, it was given to me.

Now I was really proud of that pistol, thinking that it looked marvelous at my side. Jimmy Thomas and I were playing in front of his house – Both well armed. Two teenage girls walking down the sidewalk commented on my gun. Anxious to share my treasure, I proudly drew my barrel-less weapon from it scabbard. They broke out in laughter. Today I realize what a truly funny sight that must have been, but then it just hurt.

All I recall of V-J Day is the bells of the churches ringing and there was excitement everywhere. I understand that there was a storm or fire siren sounded in Stigler, but I can only recall the bells.

Daddy was discharged and returned some months later. I was thrilled to see him. He hugged James and me, gave me two dimes to take James and get some ice cream at the drug store. Instead, we walked to Boone School and played on the equipment.

Then, we bought cokes and a candy bar at the Stigler 5 and Up. I took James home and I went to Mema Mac's for a game of marbles.

Again, my dad and I passed each other without connecting.

THIRTEEN

After returning from World War II, Daddy had gotten a job in Miami, Oklahoma. Using the training he received in the Army Air Corp, he repaired radios and other electrical appliances.

We rented a house at 127 NE "B" Street. The house was rural art deco, beautiful quartz stones and colored glass with marbles pressed into the concrete forming vines and roses. I was proud to be living in a house that I considered so beautiful.

My eldest granddaughter, Emily, and I visited the decaying shell of this house in 2004 when I drove her to a Regents meeting on the NEO campus. Only the outlines and some fragments of the colored glass remained. Nonetheless, you could detect its former shapes, shapes I thought to be so beautiful as a child. Emily indulged me, patiently following the outlines.

We had moved to Miami the summer before my fourth grade year, the summer of 1946. James was to enter first grade in Miami. A required pre-school physical detected that James had a heart murmur of some type. The local physicians after some time offered a diagnosis of Rheumatic Fever and the initial treatment was bed rest. The back bedroom, something of a long enclosed porch with lots of windows, was arranged to hold his hospital bed.

James wanted a b-b gun and Daddy got him one, set a cardboard box with a target at the other end of the room. James blazed away! I would periodically be called upon to gather the spent b-bs for reuse and change the targets.

The Stigler schools must have been rather accommodating to me. I recollect during the year I attended school in Miami (4th grade) my teacher was quite perplexed that I had so little interest in making visual identifications of the "great works of art", but was annoyingly inquisitive as to why someone would create them. The teacher sent a note home with me stating that I should ask fewer questions and listen more.

Still and all, I liked Miami. I learned that if you express your anger by knocking a baseball out of your backyard, across the alley and through a church window. A conversation with the preacher is required.

Which brings me to another religious experience; Mema Lane had come to visit us. During her stay, there was a tent revival being held a few blocks from the house. She expressed a desire to attend and I was appointed to accompany her. The topic was from the Book of Revelations. I will testify that this tent evangelist scared the holy bejesus out of me, not to mention providing me with several weeks of nightmares, and obviously creating a lasting impression.

Despite a summer long polio scare, I was allowed to walk the few blocks to the Coleman Theatre for an occasional afternoon movie. There was a period of time that this too was limited as the polio outbreak was reported to have intensified.

Increasingly, most evenings now, I read.

The antagonism I had felt toward my father for leaving us had dissipated. We talked some until James became ill, after that I simply felt more alone. So, I read even more.

It is odd the things you remember, but I recall Mother coming into my bedroom well after my bedtime and turning on the radio because Lux Radio Theatre was airing Mary O'Hara's Thunderhead. It was a book that I had read multiple times. And it was the Christmas of my chemistry set.

It seems that James was not making progress, though I am unclear as to what constituted progress. Regardless, a decision was made to take him to the Mayo Clinic in Rochester, Minnesota. I believe Dad quit his job to go with James and Mother. Granddaddy along with Nolan and Sherwell (Timmons) were providing the financial support for such an undertaking. I went to stay with Ed and Mary King to complete the school year in Miami.

A truck came from Stigler and moved the furniture from our Miami home, taking it back to Stigler. For some reason, Ed and Mary drove me to the house as the truck was being loaded.

When school was out a few weeks later, Ed and Mary took me to the bus station. I rode the bus to Stigler to be reunited with James and my parents who were staying at Granddaddy and Grandmother McBride's home.

As I said Mother and Dad had already returned to Stigler with James. They were living with Grandmother and Granddaddy, James' sick room was established in the middle bedroom.

I had not seen James in several months and he looked so frail that it troubled me; no it more likely frightened me. He was being treated with a then newly obtainable drug, penicillin, which came in a powder form to be mixed with sterilized (boiled) water. The prepared penicillin was injected into his buttocks and legs several times a day. By the time I arrived, those areas of his body were already sore, red and angry looking.

James would cry and then sob for a while after each shot. This had to be extremely difficult for Mother and Dad who administered the injections.

After a few days, I decided to walk the coward's path and stayed away as much as possible. I certainly tried to be gone during "shot times" – and those came at least 4 times a day. At first I just wondered about the town, spending time between the Boone school playgrounds and the street curbs, often with Jimmy Thomas.

Tuesdays I always seem to have the money to go to the sale barn at the fairgrounds and have a hamburger at the small wooden café there.

Granddaddy, possibly sensitive to my dilemma, was always suggesting new methods of fishing the creeks and bought me that red bicycle with the balloon tires. I was especially successful with a couple of white flies that he bought somewhere. The great success was a flat wooden spool with fishing line wrapped about it that fit nicely in my pocket and that first white fly. This allowed me to walk as far up a creek as I wished and then cut a flexible limb from a tree, notch the end slightly and tie on the line and fish away. Modified fly-fishing.

And a brand new bright red baseball cap. The cap became discolored with from being dipped into a creek and placed back upon my head on those hot summer days. I suppose it took on rather a unique dirty orange color, but it was always bright red to me.

Mema Mac would see that I left in the mornings with a can of sardines or Vienna sausage, a package of peanuts (chocolate melted to quickly) and a canteen of water. Granddaddy used to tease her that if she could find a way to get a potato patty into my pocket, she'd do it.

I always told Mother and Mema Mac my intentions for the day, which creek. Then the only requirement was that I was to leave my bicycle by the bridge and pointed in a manner to indicate which direction I had gone, up or down the creek. I don't really know why because no one in the family except Vivian and Hubert owned a car. I would spend my days that summer walking the banks, occasionally napping in the shade, and fishing the muddy waters of those Haskell County creeks.

For whatever the reason, I always fished alone. I still find comfort and see a tranquil beauty that eludes most in the small muddy creeks of eastern Oklahoma.

I slept on a pallet in the living room floor. James, who was still supposed to be on bed rest, would slip out of his bed and come lay with me. I would scratch his back and tell him stories from books I had read, about my days, about the creeks and about Stigler. I know that he liked the fishing stories.

Not long after Granddaddy had fixed the pocket spool for my line, I caught 4 really nice perch. I had strung them on a forked limb and carried them home. Mother and Mema Mac cooked them for James and me. James loved to hear the story of that day of fishing in detail; over the months I enhanced the story with additional snakes and turtles.

Listening to my tales, lying in a feeble breeze stirred by an old silver fan and the scratching of his back, he'd drift off to sleep.

Mother would find us and I would be thoroughly chastised for allowing James to be there. That failing, the morning finally came that Daddy sent me to secure a branch from the willow tree. Dad was furious and I was frustrated. For the only time in my memory, Mema Mac became outraged – It seems at both of us. I know she scared me when she started to cry. I was never again sent to the willow tree.

I cannot believe that we all were not aware that James would only come back the next night. To say Mother and Dad had become overprotective of him and remained so for the rest of his life would be a sizeable understatement.

But had the penicillin not worked, had he died, I know that I would have felt that his death was at least in part my fault. Nevertheless I also believe those nights lying on that pallet, hearing my tales of Stigler while having his back scratched may have been the only real pleasure in his life at that time.

Laying on that pallet in my Grandparent's living room was the only time during James' illness that I did not feel helpless. And it eased the guilt I felt for leaving him during the days. Even though it was James' illness that brought us back to Stigler, I was glad to be back. Back to where I could ride my new bike to the creeks or walk the railroad tracks to Canadian River, to fish the creeks, gather arrowheads at creek bank sites and search for fossils in the shale banks left by the strip miners, to the teachers I so liked and the freedom to roam the town. And, most of all, I was back with my Grandfather.

The penicillin worked its wonders and James did get well. At least he recovered from the disease. I'm not sure he ever recovered from the overindulgence that the disease spawned.

When James' death did occur on September 30, 1987, at age 47, the diseases that killed him had their genesis was in this illness and this recovery. Such is my belief.

I do know how painful the loss of my brother was to me even though I am acutely aware that in many senses I had long before lost him to alcohol. The pain was enhanced because his death came at time that he and Wilma had moved to Tulsa. I had hope.

I still find comfort in the knowledge that while I had dropped in for about a half-hour visit before coming home, it was my youngest son, Michael, who had a lengthy visit with my brother in the hospital the evening before he died. When I talked to James just before the evening news, Michael's visit seemed to have reinvigorated him. Again I had hope.

It was about mid-morning and I was at Cascia Hall (School) when the call came from St. John, saying that a code had been called and he was in crisis. Dread replaced hope.

When I arrived at his room, the Doctors and the staff were struggling in an attempt to revive him. This sight will always remain one of my most aching personal experiences. Strange, I remember wanting so badly to yell at him to breathe – but I couldn't make a sound. I could only see the paddles on his chest and the frantic movement around him. Hope to regain my brother in this life left me.

Dr. James Green, our family physician, put his arm around my shoulder, took me from the room, and said, "There are people who will need you today".

Wilma, my brother's wife, and Billie were seated in a dictating cubicle. I wish I could remember what I said to Wilma, but I can't.

Billie and I came directly from St. John Hospital to our home. Mother and Dad had just arrived. I met them beside the dining room table, their looks ask the question, and I could only shake my head no. I still could not give voice to his death. I remember the expression of utter helplessness in my mother's face. She seemed to be pleading with me to somehow do something. It was my family role to prevent such things from happening.

Daddy was standing behind her and by the time I looked to him he had turned, going into the bathroom. While he quickly emerged to hold Mother, I don't think we actually spoke until later.

As with my Grandmother Lane, my parents never recovered from James' death, from the loss of a child.

This was again a day that I knew how extraordinarily well I had married.

Now, the anger I first felt has long since faded. I miss the promise of my brother and I think of him often. I now think mostly of the good things we shared. And at times, when an event occurs that I believe he would have enjoyed, that I would like to have shared with him – Well, again as then, I just hope.

FOURTEEN

Now committed to a life in Stigler, Daddy had opened a radio repair and electrical business in some space he shared with a local plumber, Tommy Fitzgerald. He bought a Model A Ford that had a small wooden flat bed on it for service calls. He had a work bench built and placed in one corner of the sheet metal building. He was to use that bench for the entire time that he operated an electronic repair shop in Stigler. When he was focused to the task, Daddy was very talented.

Granddaddy and Mema Mac deeded Mother and Dad the lot and a half to the west of them. Granddaddy drew the house plans and contracted a builder, Preacher Roberts, to construct the home. He set strict specifications as to lumber, depth of footings, etc. We continued to live with them while the house was being built on the lots next door.

When Granddaddy would arrive home from the store, his first action would be to go into his small shed and come out with a short handled sledge hammer that someone had make for him at an earlier time.

I would be on his heels by the time he left the shed. He would inspect all of the construction from the day. Any materials or workmanship that he felt did not meet the standards that had been agreed upon felt the impact of his hammer. I know this practice irritated Preacher.

A time came that as we began our nightly inspection; Preacher drove up and was visibly angry. Granddaddy scooted me out of earshot, but not out of eyeshot.

Preacher towered over him. Still there they stood engaged in a forceful conversation with only inches separating their faces. I can still remember Granddaddy's face tilted upward and Preacher bent at the neck. In my mind it stays as a Norman Rockwell illustration.

I never knew what was said. But they both walked over to look at the day's work, discussing a number of pieces of lumber and after both nodded their heads Granddaddy's hammer knocked the 2x4 in question loose from the framing. I rushed back down for the rest of the inspection. After that day, Granddaddy did his inspection with a wax pencil he brought home from the store. He marked the material he felt was questionable. If Preacher agreed, the board was removed. This much I know, to paraphrase Billie, "The house had good bones."

Granddaddy's obsession with high quality construction did not always produce the desired result. He envisioned a canoe that would allow him and Dad to fish the Club Lake, strip pits and streams such as the Mountain Fork, and last a lifetime. There was this custom-made canoe that he had built with highest quality marine plywood available, sealed and resealed. Modeled from a picture he saw in Field and Stream, the resulting canoe was so strong, so indestructible, that I believe it could have been certified seaworthy. It also was so heavy that this two seated canoe took two men (or full sized boys) just to launch it. It was so water-tight that it rode very high in the water requiring considerable balance to fish from it. James and I enjoyed tipping it over when the other was least expecting it. And you would then have to bank the canoe in order bring it upright again.

I'm certain both David and Michael remember the canoe sitting on the north side of Mother and Dad's house, turned upside down and quite weathered. Dad finally sold it a few years before his death. I hope that it is still afloat in some water's near Stigler and some young boys are enjoying tipping each other over. However, I suspect it is sitting beside someone's home, having given up on trying to use it but not wanting to turn loose of such a finely constructed watercraft.

Granddaddy had generally quickly embraced the technology of his time, with the exceptions of driving an automobile and the dial telephone.

It seems he bought one automobile, backed it out of the yard into a tree, took it back to the dealer and got his money back. He never owned another car.

The dial telephone came to Stigler in December of 1949. While he liked the idea of the convenience of it all, he questioned the loss of the operators.

"Central." You called and ask, "What time is it?" or "Where's the fire?" When the spring sky to the west would take on the dark and ominous look, you called and ask, "Is it storming in Eufaula?" If the operator did not already know, she would find out and call you back. If you ask for someone who wasn't home, you would often be told that and where the person was – and about what time you should try again. It was this lost of personal contact – almost of community – that concerned him. I know he and Dad Bankhead, who was Mayor of Stigler at the time, had these discussions. Granddad really valued those operators and the service they provided. Of course, you could still dial O and find out about the weather in Eufaula, but it wasn't the same.

Commercial aviation he couldn't wait to try. At the first excuse, he flew to the market in St. Louis. He was completely enamored with idea of flying. Although the Sales representatives would continue to either set up displays in the Severs Hotel in Muskogee or to come to Stigler to secure his orders as they always had, he wanted to fly.

His adored Cardinals were on the road, but he went to Sportsman's Park for a St. Louis Browns game. They were playing the Philadelphia A's and he got a glimpse of Connie Mack in his business suit and with his rolled scorecard. Granddaddy was thrilled.

If it were new, he'd try it, but if after a fair trial he found it somehow lacking, he'd discard it. He thought that nylon shirts, which would not require wives and mothers to iron them, were going to be wildly popular. Then, he discovered how hot they could be as they trapped the heat next to the body on a humid Oklahoma summer day.

He had other misadventures with technology. During the late 1940's, as A.W. Hays of Muskogee, his friend and business partner's health begin to yield to a lung disorder, A.W. would journey to Albuquerque, New Mexico where he professed that his breathing was easier. He would stay at the Harvey House near the railroad tracks. Matters of business would take Granddaddy, by bus to Muskogee and then train to Albuquerque, to consult with Mr. Hays. On a summer visit, Granddaddy became enthralled with the evaporative coolers that worked so well in that dry desert climate.

A few years previous, he had installed a huge attic fan in his home with a timer that would automatically shut it off in the early hours of the morning. On his return to Stigler, he began to design a window box that could take advantage of the breeze the fan create. What a great wind that fan could create!

The frame was 2x4 with a fine wire screen on both sides. It was filled with particular straw-like crate packing that he felt resembled the material that he had seen on the sides of the evaporative coolers. At the top, he had placed a sheet metal trough that resembled guttering. He had holes punched in the bottom of it to allow the water to trickle down into the compressed packing which was held in place by the screen wire. He installed his "chiller" in the window located between his chair and Mema Mac's chair in their setting room.

A hose would be turned on low filling the tray, allowing the water to soak the packing. As the attic fan pulled the air through it did produce a cooler air, but the force with which the fan drew the air through the padding would send droplets of water into the room, striking an unsuspecting victim.

The attic fan's movement of the air also dried the padding more rapidly that Granddaddy had anticipated. In an attempt to correct this design flaw, he would send the first available grandchild to take the hose and dampen the padding. Most often me, as James had quickly learned that he could irritate Granddaddy no end by standing close to the window with the garden hose and spraying the water with all the force a depressed thumb could muster directly upon the padding, sending even larger droplets of water to sailing into the setting room. This would create something resembling a rainstorm.

Mema Mac, understanding that this creation was not soon to leave her window, insisted that Granddaddy bring oilcloth home from the store to cover her cherished chairs.

Granddaddy persisted until summer's end, then had his "chiller" carefully removed from the sitting room window, stored it in the shed. He then declared it to be a success.

It was not placed in the sitting room window ever again.

FIFTEEN

In early 1948, Daddy moved his shop to a space near the center of town. It was small, but unlike his place at Fitzgerald's, it had a gas heater. The entry door was just off the side walk and faced the back door of Zenus Garland's Domino Parlor. Between the doors was a staircase leading to the office of W.D. Hargis, a local insurance agent.

Daddy felt that this location made it a real business and there needed to be someone in the shop during business hours. Every day after school, I stopped and if there were service calls to be made, I was left to answer the phone, let people retrieve their repaired appliance or leave an appliance to be repaired. At times, after an appliance was left, I would do the simple things like changing plugs or rewiring lamps. But mostly, I would read and do whatever home work I had.

The domino hall presented a source of immediate gratifications. The Coke case, restocked and re-iced each morning, was certainly an attraction. The clatter of the dominoes and the laughter presented an agreeable backdrop.

The unlighted staircase was a more daunting matter. Its walls had not been painted in some time and much of the paint that existed was peeling from for plaster walls. The stairs themselves worn past any possibility of identifying if they had ever been painted, leaving them with the weather-aged grey look of exposed wood. Years of use had left a clear well-worn path in the wood.

But it was the man who climbed those stairs each morning who intrigued me. W.D. Hargis was so very slender that it made him appear taller than he actually was. His movements appeared deliberate, fluid yet forced. There was joylessness to his movement.

When I first encountered him, he so perfectly matched my visualization of Ichabod Crane from the Legend of Sleepy Hollow that I kept my distance. I suspect that at least subconsciously I imagined the "headless horseman" might be concealed at the top of the staircase.

When I ask about him, I was just told that he was a very kind man and to be polite to him.

That was the pattern, until one summer day, I had gone back to the shop after lunch while Dad ran a quick service call. I was seated in my usual spot near the door. Mr. Hargis was returning from his lunch, I kept reading but as always was quite aware of his comings and goings. He took a couple of steps up the stairs, came back and entered the shop. I suspect I looked rather startled. He smiled and placed a dime in my hand and said, "When your Dad gets back, go into Garland's (the domino hall) and get us both a coke and bring them up."

About mid-afternoon, I went up that staircase, Cokes in hand, likely more slowly and deliberately than Mr. Hargis ever did. The office reflected the man and his time; the plain wooden furniture was old, sturdy and well-worn. From that office was a view of the intersection of Main and Broadway. While conceding that it was the only intersection in Stigler of any commercial consequence, I thought it was a site to behold.

This was the first of many Cokes and conversations I would share with the quiet, soft-spoken man during the next two years. Most often we talked about the simple things of Stigler life, watching the people come and go – who went into the Palace Drug and who went into Bell's Pharmacy, who was getting a haircut from Sam Keith or Walter Lewis – and I always liked the fact that we where higher than the marquee of the Time Theatre. He liked to talk about the Isaac Walton League and tell of how he came to lease the club lake. He loved fishing and hunting, but as best I could tell he rarely did them any longer.

After a time, with considerable hesitation, he began to mention his son, a son that I did not know he had, and a son who carried his name. He spoke of things they might have done when his son was about my age. He only once told me that he lost his son in World War II.

As I begin to inquire of others, it seems that Mr. Hargis' son was the first man from Haskell County killed during World War II. The story that I would hear was his son's aircraft left Hamilton Field, California on the evening of December 6, 1941 and was destroyed December 7, 1941 while attempting to land during the Japanese attack on Pearl Harbor.

Years later, Boots Claunts would tell me W.D. Hargis, the son, came to Tulsa with Boots and Roland Hill to enlist with the cadet recruiter at Spartan School of Aviation. It seems that W.D. was some 4 to 5 pounds under the minimum weight. The recruiter told him to go eat bananas and come back just before the office closed at 4:30. Boots gives an account of sitting on the curb somewhere on Route 66 where they had a view of the Philtower Building with Hargis eating all the bananas they could collectively afford. He went back at 4:30 and "made the weight". And was the only one of three accepted into the Cadet Training Program.

Mr. Hargis and I enjoyed each other greatly. When as he would say I left for a "real job" at Hays and Buchanan, James replaced me on shop duty. As much pleasure as he might have found in our conversations and our friendship, he would come to love James.

I could become absorbed in Mr. Hargis stories, but James shared his passions. He got James a subscription to Field and Stream and they spoke of the stories as if they were Biblical in nature. This was a subscription that he renewed each year until James completed high school.

I like to believe that Mr. Hargis found a bit of optimism during those visits with me. But I believe he found such tangible reminders of his son in James that he treasured their talks.

I know this for certain; Mr. W.D. Hargis enriched my life and the life of my brother.

SIXTEEN

No matter how skilled the observer, there is knowledge that can only be acquired through actual experience.

It was a perfect summer Sunday. Jimmy Thomas' dad, Lucian Thomas who owned and operated the local Western Auto, was taking James Fisher, Jimmy and me to the Mountain Fork creek to swim.

Our first stop was to go across the tracks to the ice house. We bought our block of ice and placed the block in the chopper so that chunks of ice dropped into the cooler covering our cokes. Then our sandwiches, wrapped in wax paper, where placed on top of the ice.

The swimming hole at Mountain Fork was a wonderful and exciting place. It was a large pool of clear water. There had long been a rope swing tied to a large tree on the west bank of the creek. This allowed you to swing out over the creek, dropping into the water when you turned loose of the rope.

On this Sunday we had taken a special toy, a very large glass jug of adequate size that a boy could lay across it, floating so that the soft current of the stream would carry you from the north end of the hole to the south end.

We would change into our swim suits beside the car on the east side of the stream, race down the slope to the creek and swim across to the bluff with the rope swing. The rope swing was exhilarating, it seemed so daring. The expertise needed was to time your release to the highest point, dropping down into the water. Some of the more experienced boys could release, turn and enter the water head first. None in our group had attained that level of skill, but we all aspired to it.

After several trips in and out of the water, the soil and clay of the bluff would become slick requiring the swimmer to utilize the rocks and tree roots that jutted out the bank in their ascent up the bank. James Fisher was climbing out of the water when his foot slipped and he stepped squarely upon the glass jug that after a brief test upon arrival had been placed to the side until we were ready to float.

The breaking jug sounded like a gun shot. The blood spurted from just above his ankle and he fell back into the creek. I was in the water and Jimmy was above retrieving the rope swing. The blood seemed to fill the creek. I grabbed James under the arms and Jimmy came sliding down the bank. As I recall he got a very large bruise from that slide. Odd, but I remember that he looked like a pinball bouncing off the rocks and roots. We begin to tow him across the stream.

Mr. Thomas was fishing a short distance away. I suspect our yells got his attention as he met us at mid-stream. We got James to ground and Mr. Thomas took someone's shirt and quickly made a compress for what we could now see was a gapping hole in James leg just above the ankle. He told me to hold it tight and I did. After we got him into the back seat of the car, he made his belt and a piece of a branch into a tourniquet he placed just above the knee. He twisted it and told Jimmy hold it.

The drive back to Stigler was a blur even then. I held the compress as tightly as I could. I remember the numbness in my hands; then cramps followed by pain. I could see the blood covering my fingers yet did not feel it. I just held on.

Jimmy was releasing and then tightening the tourniquet upon his dad's command. The car seemed to be skidding all over the gravel road. It is the sound of the gravel sliding and the skidding that I most recall of that drive. Until, James seemed to lose consciousness. At that point, my fear made the world inside that car silent. I know Jimmy and I looked at each other on a couple of occasions, but neither of us found any reassurance. We both just held on.

Stigler having no hospital, Lucian Thomas drove his car right up to Dr. Tom's (Conklin) front door. It was his driving and his instructions that saved James Fisher that day. He stayed focused during a fearful time, keeping Jimmy and me attentive to the task at hand despite our fear.

I next recall sitting with Jimmy on the porch of that house eating a sandwich and drinking a coke. Then, I walked home.

SEVENTEEN

I do not want to leave the impression that after World War II and James' illness that my Father and I showed each anything other than respect. That would not be true. I believe we both genuinely loved each other, but we just kept passing each other in life, walking different paths. We simply fell out of touch and never really regained it.

There was always this seemingly great distance between my father and me; somehow just out of each others reach.

During my later school years, I do not recall a single direct confrontation with either of my parents until the issue of college choice arouse during my senior year. They truly did allow me to follow my own path. I had no curfew, but I was rarely out past 10. I would frequently come in from the store, eat, do what homework I deemed necessary and then leave the house to walk to whatever hangout was then in fashion, or just as often go to the gym to shoot around.

Later most evenings, I read by the light of a small reading lamp on the side of the desk that separated the twin beds in the room my brother and I shared.

I enjoyed studying, reading and listening to the radio. In later years Mother would share how it amazed her that she would hear me laugh at something on the radio and yet I would never miss a beat on a homework assignment or look up from the book I would be reading. I know it puzzled them that I continued to prefer the radio to television. I did, at the time, consider television a nuisance that created static on my AM radio.

Television! It was television that changed my parents life that the spring and summer of 1949. WKY in Oklahoma City began to transmit its picture with KOTV in Tulsa following in the fall. Daddy and Paul James of Oklahoma Tire and Supply brought a small Air King television; a brand somehow related to Hallicrafters which based upon Dad's Air Force experience he had concluded represented the highest quality electronics. In it's a blonde wood cabinet; there it sat on our dining room table.

It was mostly "test patterns and snow" but people were enchanted. It so captivated them that television antennas sprouted all over Stigler and I'm sure every other small community in Oklahoma.

It provided Dad with a rare burst of optimism. He and Paul James put their hopes in this new technology. Dad saw a future in the repair and the installation portions of the business; he was excited about it. He tinkered with that television set for hours upon end, trying to secure a dim, snowy image of the test pattern transmitted by WKY in Oklahoma City.

His belief in the future of television made him more animated and energetic that he had ever been.

These early television years marked the most successful and financially prosperous period of my Father's life.

This was the nature of our relationship until I became convinced that both Mother and Dad were enabling my brother's addiction to alcohol. They drank with him and shared with him what seemed to me to be an endless supply of painkillers Daddy obtained from the VA; in my mind enabling his addiction and making constant excuses for his conduct.

At that point, my concern and displeasure took a more tangible and regrettably a more judgmental form.

I wanted to help James but I just did not know what to do. As with the late nights on that pallet in my grandparent's living room floor, I felt powerless to actually help him. And I suspect that much of the time my help was the last thing he desired.

It would have been much easier had I not loved him so much.

PART TWO

The Soul of My Tale

EIGHTEEN

As the school term was drawing to a close in the spring of 1949, after eating Granddaddy McBride's traditional and predictable Sunday supper of Derby hot tamales with chunky French fries, which he prepared with great pride, perhaps an attempt to acknowledge the manner in which Mema McBride managed their household. After Sunday supper, the assembled family moved to the preferred conversation area, the front porch. The family conversations were as traditional as his meals, everyone, regardless of age, was encouraged to participate. His attitude toward attendance at these Sunday gatherings was the same as his belief about school attendance, it was not optional. But for as long as I could remember I hung on every word, it was like a personalized addition of the county newspaper as the stories of the people who had come to the store during the previous week flowed, a captivating blend of humor and concern.

Sunday was the only day of the week my Grandfather, "Mr. Mac" to everyone in Stigler, did not work. The store, Hays and Buchanan, opened at 7AM and Closed at 6PM except on Saturday when it remained open until 9PM. Dad's television repair shop hours were 8AM to 5PM, often followed by service calls, although to Granddaddy's concern Dad would often spontaneously close his shop, and go to make a rural service call in the Model A truck. It seemed that he often found more use for his casting rod than for his voltmeter on these calls. He would tell Mother that he would be home at "dark thirty", his fishing term for 30 minutes after dark. I know for certain that a farmer with a well-stocked pond got prompt attention.

As this evening was coming to a close, Granddad asked if I would stop by the store after school the next day. Since as best I could recall my conduct had merited no stern discussion, such an invitation could only be to my benefit. And I knew that Granddad conducted actual business only at his office in the store. However, we had had various conversations for years about the importance of work and when a boy should start to assume some responsibility.

Perhaps my first paid task was getting a quarter from Mema Mac for taking Granddad's lunch to him on Saturday, the busiest day of the week and the only day he did not walk home from the store for his lunch. I would visit with him while he ate. Of course, I understood even then my Grandmother overpaid me for such a chore so that I could pay the 10-cent admission at both theatres, The Time and The Place, for the Saturday matinees and still have a nickel for a Coke between the theatres. The theatre owners, Jack and Kathleen Pierce, did not believe in concession stands, those would only create a mess in the theatres of which they seemed so proud.

Beyond that and "babysitting" my father's shop, my chores to this point had been pleasant activities, such as standing on a stool and chipping away at the morning ice in the Coca-Cola box at the Stigler 5 & Up owned by Aunt Vivian and Uncle Hubert

(Claunts). Now give a boy an ice pick and two big blocks of ice and you have a recipe for sheer joy.

The 5 & Up was the supplier of school books for the Stigler Public School and much of the rest of Haskell County. There were no free text books until the mid-1950's, and each school had provided the 5 & up with the list of texts and "required" student supplies in the spring.

An experience that I know my Mother, Boots Claunts and I all shared in our youth took place in the late summer, the traditional stuffing of the school sacks. A paper poke (sack) was prepared containing the proper textbooks, pencils and notepaper for a student at a given school, in given grade. I don't recall exactly how many dependent rural schools there were in 1947, but there was a number. Whitefield, Hoyt, Enterprise, Martin Box, Rucker, Tamaha, Lequire, Kamina, Garland, and Perry were some.

I loved the books; new books even have their own smell. And to get to check the Reader for the next school year before anyone else was a thrill. I would sit on the cases in the back room and have the reader completed well before school opened for the fall term. I did enjoy the stories in those Readers.

It was while reading these books that I discovered that my Aunt Vivian and a couple of the other women who worked in their "husband's" stores were closet smokers – more accurately stockroom smokers, no filtered stuff, Chesterfields. Now at the time only "scarlet women" smoked, certainly not the pillars of the Southern Baptist congregation, this was their secret social pleasure.

During the summer, I'd watch from dad's shop for Elnora James and Fern Holley to make their entries for what I labeled "the afternoon smoke and coke break". I would wait until I was certain they were comfortable and then I would suddenly appear in the stock room, my coke in hand. The ladies arms would wave, scattering the smoke. Auntie would scold me as she ushered me out into the alley. And there I would sit behind the old wooden café that stood where Hoover's drug store now stands and listen to the "real country music" that made it's way from the Jukebox, I'm sure far too pleased with myself. In Stigler in the 1940's, fun was where you found it.

Between the spring day and the racing of my imagination as to what the conversation with granddad might hold, this likely was not my most productive school day.

I had study hall late in the day. Study hall was a place as well as an activity, a room filled with students ranging from 7th graders to seniors. In my memory, the room was large, seemingly almost auditorium-like with progressively elevated rows of school desks, each desk with its own unique knife-craved top and likely held together by the years of chewing gum accumulated under it. At one end, inside protective wire, was the school library.

I always rather enjoyed being able to read with the periodic comedy relief of someone rolling a marble down an aisle, we stifled our laughter at the sound and the perplexed look on the face of the poor teacher who had been assigned to monitor the study hall. In retrospective, the fact that a rolling marble would make such a sound would seem to attest to the overall quiet of this room.

A silence in which the passing of written notes required the subtlest of movements, as a note would move from student to student before arriving at its destination – and it would have been considered bad etiquette for anyone along the chain to open a note or fail to send it along its path. As I think upon it, I find it remarkable how much activity took place without verbal disruption. But on this day, even this room of books, restrained socializations and general entertainment, could not be exited quickly enough.

This was the same two-story school building, three if you count the basement, in which my parents, my uncles and aunts, had attended. I liked that. Daddy seemed to have an endless supply of study hall stories.

It was with a certain degree of sadness that I moved to the new High School after the Christmas Break of my freshman year.

I have vivid memories of that old library and I can't really recall if the new high school even had a library.

I remember literally racing to my locker, only to be delayed for a scolding by Mr. John Harmon, who viewed my enthusiastic flight as a hallway hazard. My wooden locker was just outside his door and most often I delighted in the opportunity to visit with this exceptional history teacher, always flattered that he would have a serious discussion of world matters with a seventh grader. But not today, however I did walk down the stairs and out the door, before returning to the increased pace.

By sidewalk and well-worn dirt path, covering ground at a rate that must have shocked my classmates for I was most often one of the last students to exit the building and enjoyed taking in all the sights Stigler could provide; making my way to town at a very casual pace. This day I did not even stop to watch the crew completing the installation of the poles for Stigler's first stop light, which was to hang in the middle of the only true intersection of downtown, which had over the last couple of days required at least 20 minutes of my supervision.

Into the men's side of the store, through the "hole in the wall" that had been opened to connect the adjoining commercial spaces, connecting the Ladies side of the store with the Men's side, and up the 20 steps to the office on the landing, only to find that the quickness of my arrival found Granddaddy still laboring over an order form for fall shoes, struggling to match what he believed people would buy, the quality of shoe he believed they should have, and the amount of money he would have available for shoe inventory.

Granddad methodically finished his inventory, asking an occasional rhetorical question about what I thought kids might find stylish for the fall, until he had reached some mental measure that allowed him to turn his attention to me.

As with everything else in life, Granddaddy's approach to me was straight forward and to the point. He said he thought I was reaching the age that I might be of help at the store, proposing that we give it a try on the first Monday I would be out of school. I was to undertake cleaning some areas of the store that I was soon to discover could not have been cleaned since the store's beginnings.

On Monday a new ritual would begin. Although I had my own alarm clock, Mother began to awaken at 6:00 a.m. as I did and she would fix my breakfast as I dressed for the day. We might talk some as we sat at the table, but she always waited to eat with James and Dad. To my recollection she never missed a day preparing my breakfast.

Granddaddy left for the store at 6:45 AM and I would leave the house so that I could be waiting on his steps for him. He opened the store at 7AM so "working men" could have their needs met on their way to their job. On that very first morning, there was a man on his way to work for the railroad waiting at the door to buy a pair of leather Wolverine work gloves.

After Granddaddy completed the sale, turned on all the lights and the dust covers had been removed from each merchandise counter, I was equipped with a water pail, a stack of mopping towels, and a ladder; I began my career in the world of work. I think it gave a different meaning to the concept of climbing the ladder of success.

Making more trips up and down the ladder to empty the pail of its dirty water and refill it with clean water, mopping on my hands and knees, I cleaned what seems to this day to be dirt and dust inches in depth from the wooden frame structures lining the walls, covered with oilcloth, that prevented the same dust and dirt from falling through the cracks onto the clothing hung below.

Since my return from Miami, I would often walk to Hays and Buchanan before the store closed in the evening to walk home with him, but today was different. It was with sore knees and an aching back that I walked home that evening with Granddaddy. Pride prevented me from even mentioning the aches and pains; my Grandfather never mentioned the quality of my work. However, the walk was quieter than usual, without even the usual commentary on yapping dogs at the Bell's house or the progress of Paul and Elnora James' flower garden. When we parted at his doorstep, his smile and his invitation to come up after supper told me all that I would ever need to know about that first day's effort.

My knees were still tender the next morning, but I filled my bucket and proceeded up the ladder. But having learned from the previous day's experience and giving it thought overnight, I carefully folded a towel so that it would cushion my knees.

While on the first day I saw taking a break as a sign of weakness, this second day when the cushioning of the towel wore thin, I would sit back on the ledge and gaze out over the women's side of the store. I know my grandfather took note because he mentioned that I might want to observe which aisle customers entering the store were prone to choose. I took that as a subtle message that by being observant you could learn something while appearing to do nothing. As I was later to discover, the fact that customers tended to turn to their right was important in his arrangement of merchandise.

He really enjoyed people's purchasing patterns. He took special pleasure in the handkerchiefs, the washable and reusable Kleenex of that time. You see he only bought handkerchiefs in large bundles. He'd randomly separate them into two large clusters that would be draped from the north wall of the men's department. One cluster was priced 2 for 25 cents and the other 10 cents per handkerchief. He absolutely loved to eavesdrop on the discussions of prospective customers about the relative quality of the handkerchiefs, many ultimately deciding that the 2 for a quarter ones were of visibly better quality.

I discovered that resting could be educational beyond just the business world. While taking one such break, the two ladies shopping below me where conversing about matters concerning their husbands. It was an eye-opening introduction to the concept that men and women viewed certain elements of marital life quite differently. Too be sure, I learned that women were much more talkative about intimate matters than I had ever imagined. When I had heard quite enough, I scooted my bucket and righted myself. This sent a pair of startled ladies scurrying to shop another part of the store.

At mid afternoon of that second day, the oilcloth on both ledges was clean. My back had joined my knees in considerable discomfort. Although it was never to be done again, I placed the towels and bucket neatly in the storage room to front of the men's side of the store and carried the ladder to its place in the shoe department in preparation for the next scrubbing of the ledges.

Exactly how closely granddaddy had been watching, I can still only guess, but he had his Panama hat in his hand when he met me coming back up the aisle from storing the ladder. I likely will always recall the simple words that I heard as an invitation into a more adult world, Granddaddy said, "Let's go across to the Whiteway and get a cup of coffee." As they stepped out the door, Granddaddy placed his hat on his head for the short walk to the café. There was such a great dignity to the manner in which he wore those summer hats, real Panama straws. To this day, I wish I could wear such a hat with the same style and grace that he did. Even when jaywalking to the café, Granddaddy had a gait I can only describe as a gentlemanly stroll. But it seemed to say that this man is important, even to a newcomer to the community.

The afternoon coffee in the Whiteway Café was thick and bitter, but it was my first cafe coffee. That Granddaddy was pleased with both my work and my effort thrilled me. His explanation for the two day clean up was simple, "The other folks in the store had to see you'd work before I could hire you."

I can tell you to this day that such a blend of long overheated, distilled mid-afternoon cafe coffee and affirming words were pure nectar for a boy's soul.

But first, I had to have a Social Security card. We walked from the café to the post office. I filled out the papers and handed them to the clerk. It seems that they typed the name on my card there; I signed it and left a member of the workforce.

This was very important to my Grandfather. He thought that Social Security and Franklin Roosevelt's other programs had gotten us out of the depression; these were the guidelines to a successful future. I can't really even begin to tell you the passion with which he believed this. No more state old-age pensioners, no more mills saying Old Age Assistance. I suppose he was both right and wrong.

My job description was clear, each task concrete. I'd walk with him to store each morning at 6:45, sweep the sidewalk in front of the store and wash the store front windows with a bucket of water and a squeegee, help with any lifting and carrying, maybe wait on a customer who needs something before he has to go to work. And I was to always check with him before leaving to go to home or to school. I'd come back about 4 in the afternoon to take care of any errands, especially the post office, or odd jobs, then sweep out both sides of the store before closing. Then, most days we'd walk back home together.

My pay was 40 cents an hour, I got a raise to 50 cents in the fall – after he had decided "I'd work out."

I remember feeling the flush of "wealth". Fountain cokes were a nickel at Head's Drug Store and the movies were 50 cents, now that I was over 12 years old. I could still have plenty of time most mornings go fishing in the streams or to play baseball at the fairgrounds. And on some days after work a swim in the strip pit was but a bicycle ride away.

The strip pits with their cool and clear water were the public pools of the time. I'd throw my inter-tube over the handlebars of my bicycle. Inter-tubes served not only as floatation devices for leisurely paddling around the banks, but also as diving targets from the bluffs –I'm sure those bluffs are not as high as I remember them to be – you just needed to be sure the value stem was pointing downward to avoid the scrapes and cuts as you passed through the tube. A scraped belly was the sure sign of a beginning tube diver. The favorite pit, just west of the Club Lake, has long since been filled in by some well-intended land reclamation project or another.

Life was good and I had money, liberating money!

NINETEEN

In the late 1940's major league baseball was played during the day and the minor leagues ruled the night. At the end of that first summer, a week before school started, Granddaddy, who knew that I listened to the Muskogee Reds, a team in the Class C Western Association, almost every night, gave me a bonus envelope. It contained a roundtrip bus ticket to Muskogee, a box seat ticket for two nights, a voucher for two nights in the Severs Hotel and $20.00 "meal money". It was wonderful – no, it was incredible.

So, it was a movie in the afternoon and a baseball game at night. For one lunch, I walked to the Carnation Place. It was a sandwich shop connected to the Carnation Milk Company's dairy facility, it was burgers and malts. In Stigler your ice cream selection was limited to vanilla, chocolate and strawberry – on occasion chocolate marvel – and the Carnation place had what seemed to be endless rows of different kinds of ice cream and sherbet.

The rooms at the Severs Hotel had those large fans that stood at the top of a lamp like base with a high speed that would create a breeze that would make even an Oklahoman proud. I thought these fans were amazing and dreamed of someday being able to afford such a luxurious fan in my bedroom.

While I had taken a few day trips alone to Muskogee and Fort Smith, I had never experienced anything like this.

Understand we never took a vacation until the summer before my junior year of high school. Then, we took a three-day trip through the western Ozarks, the four of us in the front (and only) seat of a new International pickup truck. Mother did love the Ozarks Mountains.

James and I entertained ourselves with a bean flip, shooting pebbles at the road signs as we navigated the gravel back roads of Arkansas. And that was entertaining!

TWENTY

This working arrangement at Hays and Buchanan was to continue with only one interruption until my high school graduation. Just prior to the Christmas break of my 8th grade year, the school, with Mom and Dad's consent, decided it would be good if I begin practicing with the varsity boy's basketball team. The classes in junior high were segregated by gender. This change required a scheduling adjustment that put me into some classes that were otherwise exclusively composed of 8th grade girls.

Granddaddy felt that all this was an unnecessary distraction from my education. Education had such immense real and symbolic value to Granddaddy. I am sure that the fact that he had, of necessity, left school at 12 year of age to work in the coal mines of Huntington, Arkansas to help support his mother and sisters played a very real role in this. He had struggled to see that three of his four children attended (and completed) college during the depths of the Great Depression. Only Daddy chose not to attend college, he and mother marrying during the Christmas break of 1935, their senior year in high school, in Greenwood, Arkansas. My parent's decision to elope was one of the rare topics Granddaddy would never discuss with me.

While Granddad was a real baseball fan and a devout St. Louis Cardinal Fan, I did not believe that my grandfather ever saw me compete in a single athletic event. I knew he relished watching the town baseball team on Sunday afternoons; before I started playing with this team at 15, we had regularly attended together. He certainly never mentioned my participation in the Sunday rituals to me. But he freely praised the talents of the local men with whom I played, crediting his knowledge to what others had told him. It was only after his death that I learned he would come and sit in "Dad" Bankhead's car down the right field line to see me play baseball. He never attended a basketball game, a football game or a high school baseball game. I am certain that he believed all school athletics were a distraction from the education for which schools were intended.

Regardless, after the Christmas of my 8th grade year, he laid me off, saying only that there would be less to do after Christmas. As soon as basketball season was over, he rehired me. After consideration, I have concluded that it was in part because the men working at the store were no longer accustomed to having to do the cleaning and carrying chores that I had been doing. He would have been sensitive to that.

Upon my re-employment, at 55 cents an hour, I began working all day Saturday, 7AM to 9 PM. In a rural county with a family on about every 80 acres, Saturday was the big shopping day and I got to work the sales floor. I got no commission, but I got a lot of credit with Granddad. Life was very good.

I was able to make some extra money in putting up television antennas for Dad. But that only lasted until my Mother saw me hanging over the eve of the two story Fears house setting a screw for a guide wire. Daddy replaced me with a man who did odd jobs around town.

TWENTY-ONE

Sometime during the summer of 1953 Granddad made a decision that would profoundly influence me, a decision that seemed incompatible with the temperament of the times and in conflict with his personal and business interest.

His decision led us to explore the discernible, yet murky elements of ourselves and of those near to us. I do not believe either of us envisioned the fragile nature of the path he had chosen at the onset. I am not certain that I understand much of it to this day. It was a choice that was certainly contradictory with his frequently espoused philosophy that expressions of a political and religious character only hurt business.

Of course, this was a man who beginning with the shortages and the rationing of World War II always had bubble gum in his pocket for every child who came into his store, regardless of where he had to get it or what he had to pay for it. He preferred Fleers with the comics enclosed, but he found nothing less than Super Bubble to be acceptable.

I would hear stories from ladies that he considered his "good customers" about when those rare shipments of nylon hose would arrive during World War II, he would telephone them. I particularly remember one lady's story of how she had declined his offer of credit when she did not have the cash at the time the shipment arrived, at least not cash budgeted for the nylons that she so badly desired. Her husband, as with many of his time, did not approve of credit. So, Granddaddy told her not to concern herself, and he held her a pair, safe in his desk drawer so there could be no accidental sale. He kept them secure in his desk drawer for over a month until she had the money to pay for them.

The shortages of the depression and the war had his attention. During the war metal clothes hangers were not available. Given the rhetoric of the Cold War and having seen two world wars, he made certain that when the next one occurred his store would have hangers. I cannot tell you how many clothes hangers I tied in bundles of 25 and carried to an upstairs storeroom or how many thousands of hangers were in that room. I have wondered what the workman who renovated the store after its sale must have thought when they came upon that room. It had to be funny and befuddling.

On any ordinary summer day, I would sit at the base of the steps leading to granddad's office landing until I heard the sound of the fan being turned off and his footsteps, signally a completed day. The conversations on our walks home were nearly always worth the wait. But this late July day, he came to the top of the stairs and motioned for me to come up.

He was already leaning back in his chair, yet somehow not appearing quite himself, rather lost in his thoughts, as I reached the office area. In retrospect, I only recall seeing him in such a solemn and contemplative mood one other time, when a few years later as we both sat in the same chairs, he told me of his cancer and what he felt was his approaching death; of his wishes.

Granddad sat at his roll top desk with his fingers tapping a familiar rhythm (when he was thinking he always tapped the same rhythm, something of a drumbeat, using all his fingers) and looked out over the women's side of the quiet and empty store, I remember the silence and orderly row of counters stretching to the front door each draped in a white cloth to protect the merchandise from dust over night. For a brief moment his gaze turned to me and then back to the store as if making some type of final assessment before speaking.

I had learned long ago never to look away from his eyes, my Grandfather's imperative, an oft-repeated observation, "Never trust a man who can't look you in eye when your talking with him." While I had often pondered that because I found that his gaze would drift away from someone, fixating on some inanimate object as he tried to focus upon a person's words free of the distractions of their movements. But it did make more sense that my Dad's trust adage, "You can't trust a man with a mustache."

"I have decided that I am going to sell goods to the coloreds from 'round here". His tone was firm and his words were clipped, he was not asking my opinion as a mental exercise for both of us as he was prone to do on other occasions. This was an advisory statement. The announcement created no concern for me simply because I was too uninformed to have a grasp of any potential ramifications of what he was telling me, so I suppose I did not register the apprehension or the surprise he might have anticipated. The plain simple fact was that I had not given colored people a lot of thought and likely never foresaw the occasion to consider such a topic.

Now I had seen colored people, as Mema Mac insisted they be respectfully called as opposed to negroes, on my occasional bus trips to Muskogee and Fort Smith, but before that summer day in 1953 I am certain that I did not know a colored person; not giving much thought to the fact that some existed nearby my everyday world. I look back and see an embarrassingly intense ethnocentricity.

I never recalled seeing a black person in Stigler. I knew that the owner of the farmer's market across the alley, out the back door of the store, purchased produce, chickens and eggs from residents of Lewisville, an all black rural community near Kinta. Still I don't believe that I had ever actually spoken the simplest of greetings to a colored person.

Regardless, Granddad seemed to feel there was some principle involved that I didn't immediately grasp. I still remember just nodding in agreement as he explained to me the plans for the construction of a sitting area, benches to be more exact, just inside the back door that was just across the alley from the farmer's market.

In retrospect, this decision was inconsistent for the man who believed that the public expression of a religious belief or a political view was poor business practice.

There was no dressing area because beyond shoes, no clothes would be tried on. Shoes were always different.

For a person to have correct fitting shoes was one of the most important elements of selling clothing from my grandfather's prospective. I was to gather the requested items in a cotton pick sack (There is some symmetry there I suppose), as discreetly as possible, and return with them to the waiting customer. The re-stocking of items was to require a similar discretion.

Granddaddy rarely offered an explanation for a decision, but as I got up from the chair, he said, "I need to do what is right." Following a period of thoughtfulness, completed with a deep sigh, he continued, "This is necessary." The necessary part escaped me until many years later.

Almost as an afterthought, he added, "You do understand why I can't ask any of the other help to do this?"

I said I did, but I really didn't. I would do it simply because my Grandfather requested it of me. That you can only count on family was a mantra that I had often heard from him, so I just assumed that this was the logic and that was enough for me to know.

I suppose because I accepted his decision with so little concern that I honestly have few recollections of those early commercial exchanges. But I know that the "rear of the store rule" was short lived. It seems to me that the first time there was question about the fit of little boy's shoes due to some abnormality in the bone structure of his foot, he was taken to the X-Ray machine in the shoe department to insure correct fit.

An X-Ray machine for the purpose of insuring a correct shoe fit and yes it was X-Ray. You put your feet in the slot at the bottom and pushed the button. There before you eyes was an X-Ray of your foot. Over the years of its existence we X-Rayed broken hands, elbows and almost anything else that could be fitted into the opening. We had a recreational X-Ray. Of course, that was well before the concerns that brought on lead aprons and such.

I do recall a time that I was asked by a man who always seemed to be of some stature (and girth) about Big Smith jeans. Now understand Granddaddy felt all other denim products were inferior to Big Smith. Plus, there was a long standing loyalty to the Big Smith representative and such relationships were very important to my Grandfather.

The man noted that I had on Big Smith jeans and he asked if I'd rather be wearing Levi's which were so popular with the other boys. I can remember telling him, "Yes, but my grandfather doesn't sell Levi's, so I wear Big Smith." And I do believe they were better jeans than the Levis, just not the fashion right then. It was all about that red tag and the man allowed that was "a very high price for a little piece of red cloth." After trying on a pair of jeans, this large customer, a really big man, decided that Big Smith overalls might be the better option for him. He relayed the story of the Big Smith jeans to my Grandfather. The story pleased my Grandfather.

I fitted Wolverine work shoes and Wolverine leather gloves, cut oilcloth (for covering table and windows) and learned about piece goods.

I remember a special lady who could cut patterns from brown paper after "eye balling" the garment. At first she brought brown paper bags with her from which she had tried to smooth the creases, and then I started providing her with brown wrapping paper. The smooth brown wrapping paper brought a huge smile to her face and frequent nods of approval for me. After a few of those nods she could have had a whole roll of wrapping paper if she had asked for it. She didn't really draw anything on the paper; she just took out her scissors and cut the pattern while looking at the dress, blouse or skirt. I would bring swatches of materials or bolts at times for her examination. She would then tell me how many yards of material were needed. I suppose she was almost right. I never questioned her judgment in such matters.

I would talk sports with the men, mostly baseball. The hot stove league still flourished. Baseball was king, so no conversation about baseball was trivial or superficial. The conversations were more often about the Negro leagues, of which I found I was woefully ignorant, as about the Negro players now in Major League Baseball. I felt that while they wanted these Major League players to succeed there was clearly an element of mistrust. Often the concern expressed was about the impact such players would ultimately have on the Negro Leagues. With that said, it was still almost all business. At that most basic level, these sales transactions were little different than any other.

Most of the employees simply acted as if nothing was going on. I guess it was close to the original "don't ask, don't tell" policy. But every employee in the store certainly knew. I later learned from Clem Gibson, what a nice guy and certainly the most accepting of a boy in a man's world, that the men were just relieved that Granddaddy hadn't chosen them. It was exactly what Granddaddy had suspected. Knowing my Grandfather's determination and persistence as they did they were convinced that if it were not for me, it certainly would have been one of them who would have been asked to do this job that none of them would have relished.

Some years later, the lady who was the bookkeeper at the time spoke of another ingredient of this decision. Business in Stigler was down some and Granddaddy didn't want to have layoff any of his people.

I suspect the men all had some prospective on the state of the Haskell County economy. There were a couple of ladies on the women's side that had different opinions, but on the whole they kept their own counsel. They just were not as helpful to me as some of the other ladies. And gathering ladies things was certainly an area in which I needed assistance, a great deal of assistance. Men's sizes always seemed quite direct and straightforward while women's sizes were veiled in mysterious and illusory numbers.

After some long forgotten incident as we walked home one evening, I remarked to Granddaddy that they (the Negroes) didn't appreciate what he was willing to do for them.

He replied, "Why should they? We're making the money, not them." After a pause, he added, "A customer is a customer."

But even today when I assess a situation, I still remember to consider who's making the money. I think it has recently become popular to say, "Just follow the money."

Nevertheless we sold merchandise. No one was laid off. A door was cracked open, even if it was a back door.

I have come to believe that genuine social change comes from a compilation of rather small transactions conducted between quite ordinary men and their motivations for engaging these transactions has little to do with any overt desire for social change.

TWENTY-TWO

I stirred, reluctant to leave the sleep induced by a late Saturday evening, as an odor lightly drifted in through the window I had opened the evening before to enjoy in the mild chill of the October night. I can only assume that some area of my preconscious grasped the smell of smoke. I came up with a start. Not yet fully awake, I bumped my head on the window frame as I pressed my nose toward the screen to better smell.

It is strange how you can remember something such as the feel of screen wire on your nose, the smell of burning grass and kerosene can become so distinctive. I believe I only really became alert when I pressed my nose into the screen wire.

My eyes opened to the flames, Granddaddy's front yard was on fire. The blaze seemed to rise vertically from the ground while trails of burning grass crept in all directions, encroaching further into Granddaddy's front yard. Grabbing my jeans from my desk chair, hopping to get them on and yelling for Dad at the same time, I hit the door and after almost falling off the porch, and hit the grass running. Out the front door into the yard toward the old hydrant that protruded from the yard, several feet above the ground, I ran.

I got the hose, which had been disconnected for fear of an early freeze, from where it lay coiled next to the old home. I remember not being able to screw the hose in place as fast as I felt was needed, removed the brick that kept the outdoor facet handle hidden so that mischievous boys did not turn it on some night. Connected, I turned the water on.

I remember a sense of impaired awareness, as if it wasn't happening, as the fire took form. A cross, crude but distinct, a fire in the shape of a cross was burning. Here in Stigler, in my granddaddy's yard. I closed my thumb over the end of the hose creating a spray, dousing the portion of the fire between Granddaddy's front steps and me.

As I approached, I saw my Granddaddy outlined against a cedar tree. I saw a slight slump to his stance that I had never seen before. He snapped upright when he saw me.

His directions came simply, almost without emotion, "Wet all this by the cedars first. Then soak it over near the porch. Then let it burn. Don't waste water on it."

For whatever reason, I could not simply let the fire burn. I doused each arm of the fire that started to move from the middle of the yard.

I worked my away around the edges until another instruction came, "Let that south part burn to sidewalk that should stop it there."

I got the first whiff of kerosene. To the day of this writing, I can still recall the sights and smells of this fire.

The grass now smoldering with an occasional ember still glowing hot, I came to sit on the porch steps. Dad had arrived unnoticed while I was hosing the grass fire. The two men had sat silently until I came and sat beside them.

I ask the only question in my mind, “Why?”

I know Daddy responded with the “N” word and a reference to Granddaddy being a “pig-headed son of a bitch”. Daddy seemed to scream without raising his voice. I think now that it reflected a quiet desperation, a search for affirmation that marked a great deal of his life.

The anger I first felt toward Dad for yelling at Granddaddy melted into sadness and disappointment.

Dad went home. Outlined in the dim of our front porch light, I could see Mother and James, really just familiar silhouettes.

Granddaddy looked at me and said, “I think he does the best he can.”

I took the seat beside my Grandfather that Dad had vacated. Momentarily, Mema came out with a cup of coffee for him and a Dr. Pepper for me. Dr. Pepper and cinnamon toast, usually blackened around the edges by the time she retrieved from the oven broiler, were her cures for all ailments, physical or mental.

She took her hand and brushed his hair into place, it was a rare glimpse of his hair in any form of disarray.

I suppose trying to reassure me, Granddaddy said, “You know this is not about you.”

I said, “Its okay.” He forced a strained smile and put his arm on my shoulder. I felt like it was about us. I was confused and saddened.

As I sat there with him, trying to absorb what had happened, I began to think more about what had not happened. The

Volunteer Fire Department did not make an appearance and no neighbor crossed the street, even to express some level of concern or curiosity as what might have happened. It seemed that I had seen lights in their windows, but I am not really certain. I started to ask him, but he was deep in his thoughts. The set of the jaw registered all the answers I needed. It was characteristic of our family.

Granddad was most extroverted while he worked in the store, but his only real friend was Roy "Dad" Bankhead. To him, beyond his job, family was all anyone should need. Family burdens, as with family joys, were to be managed by the family. Still the Volunteer Fire Department's absence really puzzled me. These volunteers were good men. I now suspect it was as simple as no one called to report the fire.

I remember looking across the street and realizing that I really missed my life-long friend, Jon Conard, who was now away attending Oklahoma A&M (now Oklahoma State).

When I went back to the house and crawled into my bed, James ask, "Want a back scratch?" I laughed. James laughed. His offer reminded me of a unique bond between us, of a seminal time we had shared, and my brother's offer made me feel better.

I suppose I had no idea he still remembered the back scratching as comforting until the night of grass fire. To this day I need to believe that had I said yes, he'd have scratched my back on that night.

The next morning, even though it was Sunday, Mother was up early and cooking my breakfast. But that was her way. Whatever concern she felt, she kept her own council, but still in her silence she communicated her concern. I suspect that it assured her of always being in agreement with Dad. "Whatever Pop says."

But she had been, as always; already up when I awakened with breakfast well underway. I suppose out of habit now I got up earlier and ate before James and Dad would arouse. For all those years, Mother prepared two breakfasts, one for me and another later for James, Dad and herself. At times, she would sit with me, rarely volunteering conversation beyond inquiring about the evening past or the day ahead.

After eating, I went to survey my grandparent's front yard, although I recall glancing out my window, feeling twinges of discomfort, before leaving my bed.

George Cooper, the City Marshall, driving what passed for a police car in Stigler, parked in front. He nodded to me as he walked up on the porch and knocked on the door. Granddaddy stepped out and I positioned myself so that I could hear. I only remember that Granddaddy told him nothing had really happened, just another grass fire. I'm not sure if Marshall Cooper was perplexed or relieved by my grandfather's declaration. I can think of no reason why Marshall Cooper would wish to treat it as anything more than "just a grass fire" beyond the personal pride this man took in his position. I would later discover that the Marshall did nose around a bit.

That was the instruction Granddaddy would give me. He felt that it was "nothing unless we chose to make it something." If we made an issue of it, it would discourage whoever had fashioned the cross of kerosene and lit it from "bragging about it".

I liked Marshall George Cooper and I think he liked me. It had to be the summer of 1947. I was in the alley the day the community decided they needed a Marshal and that George Cooper was the man for the job.

I had just came out the back door of the Stigler 5 and Up, coke in hand, and was headed to sit behind the small frame café that was on the property where Hoover drug now stands. I would sit, drink my coke and listen to the country music from the café's jukebox.

I heard a very loud pop. It startled me and I ducked back in behind the wall. George Cooper joined me. A returning veteran by the name of Kirby Stevens was in the alley across the street between what was then the post office and Frix Grocery.

Kirby had, as I recall the story, a .45 caliber handgun that he had brought home from the war with him and had become delusional (I'm suspect we'd call it PTSD today). Regardless, he was firing the gun and walking down the alley. George Cooper shushed me with his finger to his lips, he listened, and then he pointed to me and with an open palm made a clear motion for me to stay put. To a frightened 10 year-old, that seemed like more than sound advice.

George left and crossed to the other side of the alley, and then I lost sight of him. I came out when I heard someone say it's over. While I have heard several versions of the story, I only know George disarmed Kirby and when I emerged George was sitting in the alley with both of his arms wrapped around Kirby, holding him securely. I simply recall Kirby crying.

Then someone telling me, "You go home boy. Your momma will be worried." On the way out of the alley several men were looking at a bullet indention in a heavy gauge cast iron signpost that was to remain there for years to come. I went home. I heard the highway patrol took Kirby to the State Mental Hospital in Vinta.

The City of Stigler had little formal law enforcement. There was the county sheriff, the highway patrol, and George Cooper was the night watchman. Shortly, George Cooper was hired as City Marshall and there he remained.

Over the years, as I saw more young men come home for wars, I never failed to remember Kirby Stevens' tears and wonder about his sadness. For some, no for most, a war never really ends.

I remember that I didn't go to church that Sunday, but I don't recall why. Whatever the reason, I still vividly recall quietly spending the afternoon listening to the New York Yankees-Brooklyn Dodgers World Series game. I was a Yankee fan, as were so many Oklahoma boys, because of Mickey Mantle and Allie Reynolds

TWENTY-THREE

To this point in life, I had always found a certain pleasure in isolation when I needed to sort things out. I first remember it being successful when Dad brought us back to Stigler from Tulsa, when he volunteered for World War II. So, I suspect my friends might have felt most comfortable keeping a reasonable distance. Anyway, no one came to talk.

The next day, in the halls of Stigler High School, not a word about the "grass fire" was spoken to me. The classrooms seemed quieter than usual, but logic dictates that they were not. No student, no faculty member or staff uttered a word, except the basketball coach, Bill Bean, who stepped up beside me as I walked down the hall way to the gym to shoot a little before football practice, patted me on the shoulder (a pat that was as close to a hug as you could get in those days) and he stammered something about Saturday night. It really didn't matter that I couldn't understand his words. The acknowledgement was enough.

The light Monday football practice seemed to drag on forever. It wasn't that I wanted to be somewhere else; I just didn't want to be there. I never regained the enthusiasm for playing football – totally unrelated; yet lost. I really enjoyed Dick Mosley, the head football coach, and continued to enjoy him.

The burned grass, with it's now erratic shape, was left to the late fall and winter rains, to the neighborhood touch football game that resumed the next Sunday afternoon. It seemed to green in the spring just as the other grass.

I know that Granddad had several very quiet conversations with Dad Bankhead, his only and most trusted friend in Haskell County, who made discreet inquiries.

Dad Bankhead just plugged along doggedly printing his weekly newspaper with less than modern equipment and offering an alternative voice to the Stigler News-Sentinel. My Granddad not only liked him, he really admired him and trusted him. Granddad would say, "He was given up as dead during the war (WWI), had been gassed, yet survived. Persistence comes easy for the man."

Granddad often told me, "You can make all the business acquaintances you want, just don't come to believe they are true friends and you won't be disappointed." Yet this was the man who so trusted people that he would give them credit as they prepared to leave for California in the spring and was never concerned about being paid upon their returned in the fall.

Within the week he did suggest that it would be a good idea if I stopped attending DeMolay, the Masonic boy's club. I did so without question and I felt no loss because I found the secret rituals quite boring and irrelevant. When other boys had ceased to be active, there was always an effort to bring them back into the fold. But my absence went unacknowledged.

But it was to remain just a grass fire. We never spoke of it again until shortly before his death.

Dad and I had only one conversation about the incident. That came in the fall of 1954, a football season in which no Oklahoma State Football Championships were determined because of strong objections to the inclusion of all-black schools (Muskogee Manual and Okmulgee Dunbar) into football districts and the playoffs.

I have noticed other explanations for this in recent years, but in Stigler in 1954 there was only one reason. I totally believe Stigler High School and their fellow NOAA conference members would have withdrawn from the State Activities Association rather than participate. Daddy saw this as justifying his position on Blacks.

Interestingly, I recall so well him saying that this trend would be "The death of the public schools". There are certainly those who today would agree that his prophecy was valid.

Three years later Daddy was elected to the Stigler School Board. At the Haskell County Historical Society there is a bronze plaque with his name that was taken from the gym constructed in about 1957.

In reflection, life was the same, yet it wasn't the same. While I still would spend time shooting snooker, pool was considered a game requiring lesser skill, with the wager of 25 cents per game plus the cost of the rack. Still it was shooting baskets that became my therapy.

A coke behind the white frame café on Main Street with the juke box playing Kitty Wells "Honky Tonk Angel" brought respite and provided an interesting observation point.

Basketball, a passion I had discovered by accidentally attending the Haskell County Grade School Tournament when I was in the third grade, became increasingly important. I could do it alone, Coach (Bill) Bean gave me a key to the gym on the condition I never let anyone else in – and I didn't although it irritated a few. But I could shoot alone, turn off the lights and then lay on the bleachers, which in the old WPA gym were permanent construction and wide, placing a rolled towel under my head. Back resting against the wood seats, head on a towel, as likely many teenagers are want to do, I reconsidered and plotted my course.

While I must confess fantasies of vengeance were certainly there, but I could not identify a person or group toward whom to direct my "well conceived, ingenious" plots.

I remember thinking about God, friends and future, not always in accepting terms.

I rarely if ever again went to the Methodist youth group, but I attended the Sunday Morning worship services regularly. Aunt Vivian had given up on persuading me to attend the Baptist Church and was now focusing on securing James' salvation. It was at the Methodist Church that there were adults I admired and trusted. There was Topsy Williams, Bo and Pauline Stumbaugh, Linus and Betty Williams, Lloyd and Edith Munn, the Conards and Opal Calhoun ---- and that brilliant high school music teacher, Mac McCrory whose solo of the Holy City was an Easter service highlight – with the choir under the direction of Louise Raney.

There is a simple comfort in the sanctuary of that Church. After my Mother's funeral, I still found the sunlight through the stained glass lily on the south wall to be extraordinary; it was especially beautiful during the winter when the sun was deeper in the southern sky and would strike at just the proper angle.

But it wasn't just sunny days; I can remember damp and rainy days when the formed concrete stone seem to yield to the rivulets that trickled down the sides of exterior walls. A strong gray building that seemed visually transfigured by the elements. I still see strength in that building.

Maybe my friendship pattern changed. While I had considerable respect for classmates like Bobby Cariker, Bill Risenhoover; for Jimmy Parker and Thomas Green who when we were boys could always gather enough of a following for a baseball game, I limited my social interactions to two friends from my earliest childhood, Jimmy Thomas and James Fisher. And then with a boy who moved to Stigler from Ft. Smith, Tommy Jeff Montgomery.

Jimmy Thomas, born a day before me, was the most loyal of friends – and I'm not certain that being my friend during those last years of high school was the easiest of task. I know he was an outstanding trumpet player, I liked hearing him play. Especially those times he would play on his front porch.

Before my senior year of high school and having met all the graduation requirements except English; understanding their practical value in the world only because my Granddad directed me toward them, I enrolled in a bookkeeping class and typing class – traditionally girls only classes. As only a very good friend would do, Jimmy Thomas enrolled with me.

Mrs. Frankie Blankenship taught both classes and we were the only two boys in those classes. Mrs. B cut us no slack because of our gender. The Underwood manual typewriters had blank keys – all black keys. I have often told other classes of students that those were the most practical classes I took in high school. I learned to type well enough to type my own dissertation on an IBM Selectric some 20 years later. I could always understand my conversations with my accountant.

The truth is I will likely never fully grasp the magnitude of my indebtedness to my teachers and my classmates in the Stigler Public Schools.

Miss Calhoun taught me to love reading, Ms. Lillian Riley and Mrs. Ruby Sewell taught me to write and no one ever succeeded in teaching me math – but God knows it wasn't from any lack of effort on their part. I did complete every math class Stigler High School offered in the early 1950's but I struggled.

Dating was fun. When trust is impaired, security can be found in diversity. So, diversity it was.

My love of Hays and Buchanan increased, I enjoyed spending time there. Working until 9 on Saturday evening might have bothered others, but it provided me with entertainment. But then again, maybe that pattern was already firmly in place.

I grew to appreciate Bill Grubbs. By this time the slump of age had begin to mark him, but still my grandfather considered him to be the ultimate suit and hat salesman. If a customer wanted to buy a suit of clothes or a Stetson hat, we were all to defer to Mr. Grubbs. This man seemed to know all there was to know about a Stetson hats and fitting suits. As he began to realize that I was genuinely interested, he started to teach me.

Also during this time in which smoking cigarettes was equated with masculinity, Bill Grubbs shared my grandfather's distain for cigarettes. But Mr. Grubbs liked his half a cigar a day. Not to smoke, he'd cut them in half and chew on one end. When a customer came in, the cigar was neatly and quickly positioned in one of his many "hiding places".

Of the things I learned from him, two really remain with me.

First and foremost was that you could not make a sale if you were not on the floor and near the front entrance. You have to be available. I believe that lesson stuck.

Second was that customers prefer and will buy the neatly folded merchandise first. So, even if another clerk makes the sale, you learn to replace merchandise to its original fold and position. I know it is difficult for my family to now believe that I might have possessed that skill.

TWENTY-FOUR

Then, in August of 1954, the good Lord let me find Billie Jean Martin, one of those pretty little Martin girls.

At the encouragement of Tommy Jeff, we went to some regional Methodist Youth Fellowship meeting at the First Methodist Church in Sallisaw. During the social time in what I think was the basement of the church, I caught a glimpse of Billie on the other side of the room. From that distance, she was pretty with such black hair against a starched white blouse with rounded collar – and she was gloriously tall. But she was gone by the time I got there.

Again as if by fate, Tommy Jeff and I stopped by Lesley's Café for God knows what reason. But sitting in Lesley's Cafe with her friend, Donna Wilson was Billie. I don't precisely recall who invited whom to sit but somebody did and we did. I will never forget those blue eyes that made such direct contact – there was no looking away.

I left with her name. It was when I tried to get a telephone number from information that the concern and consternation set in. There were Martin's but the operator said she was certain none of them had a daughter named Billie. Of course, Billie was living with her sister and her husband, Lou and Charles Mattox. After trying several times a day in hopes of finding an operator of a more cooperative bent, I finally accepted that I would wait for school to start and try the Sallisaw High School.

Then, Tommy Jeff received a saving letter from Donna Wilson whose name neither of us had been able to recall. The letter had Billie's telephone number and an invitation to call. I called and she said yes.

When Mema Mac found out that it was my plan to take Billie to the Old South restaurant in Fort Smith, she told me, "Don't order the fried chicken. (For which the Old South was renowned and I greatly liked.) No one can eat fried chicken in public and look proper." As was the custom of the time, the boy did the ordering for both. When Billie told me she wanted fried chicken, Mema's instruction went right out the window. We both had fried chicken.

It was the first of many dates that would consist of dinner at the Old South Restaurant or Constantio's and a movie at the Malco Theatre. I remember sitting in the Malco with those early 3D cardboard glasses with a green lens and a red lens and holding her hand. We enjoyed walking the streets, window-shopping in downtown Fort Smith and talking.

There were many trips over that stretch of gravel road from the Spiro Y to the Arkansas River Bridge, some very late at night.

I knew this was different from the beginning. I really wanted her to like me.

I talked to her, shared dreams with her in a manner that I had never spoken with anyone before, or since.

Mother and Dad also recognized the difference. They liked Billie, but I suppose as it became evident to them that this was not following the path of my other dating relationships I began to encounter obstructions that made dating more difficult. The 1954 Plymouth station wagon became less available.

Granddaddy said it was visible because I started leaving the store at my scheduled time on Saturday rather than staying at the store, allowing another person to go home.

It was when it came time to finalize college plans many things fell apart. While I had long been promised that I could attend any school that accepted me, such was not the case. It was only when a letter of acceptance to a school that I had long desired to attend arrived that I was told otherwise.

Then, I was told that even the University of Oklahoma was out of the question, issues developed. I believe some were rooted in the decisions they had made during their youth but I felt a real separation from my parents. Full athletic scholarships were very rare beyond the two major state universities.

My choices were limited to Connors State or Northeastern State. Further, I was not to be involved in athletics. My Grandfather and Mema Mac did not and likely could not intervene.

In retrospect, I know I should have been grateful that I could attend any type of college, anywhere. This was not even close to what I wanted, what I felt I had been promised. I was disappointed and disillusioned. Given perhaps my rather grandiose visions of the future and the fact that Billie was the first and only individual with whom I had ever completely shared those dreams, I know I was embarrassed. This was one of the rare times in my life I felt I had somehow completely and utterly failed.

I reluctantly and most unenthusiastically begin the summer of 1955 at Northeastern in Tahlequah. I quickly lost interest in school and begin quietly playing baseball in Muskogee.

Billie and I did not see each other for over 5 months. I still remember the summer and early fall of 1955 as the most miserable period of my life. I was adrift without direction until Billie and I reconnected in Sallisaw on the sidewalk outside Cheek's Jewelry.

We became engaged the Christmas of 1955. Between my savings and a loan from Granddaddy and trust me if you borrowed money from Granddaddy, even if he had offered it, you did pay it back, I was able to buy the engagement ring I wanted for her. The local jeweler assured me it was the finest in Stigler.

In March of 1956, I got a job working in the core analysis laboratory for Sinclair Research in Tulsa.

Billie and I were married in Charles and Lou Mattox home on November 21, 1956. The old house was a very large three story home with large rooms.

The altar was arranged in the dinning room area, folding chairs completed the dinning room and filled the living room. The one event I'm certain will sustain its clarity in my mind until my death is Billie coming down that staircase. I have often wished that I had the ability to actual describe what visually and emotionally I saw that Wednesday evening, her smile was brighter than the white dress she wore and she seemed to virtually float down the staircase. But I have neither the words nor the talent to do the memory justice.

And the same applies to a black baby doll gown, lacy with the crinoline.

We took a very brief honeymoon to Hot Springs, Arkansas. We moved into a one bedroom furnished apartment on North Main in Tulsa. The old wooden floor sloped toward the kitchen, but it didn't matter. Our furniture was more than just limited, but we had a 10" Crosley black and white television set that Mother and Dad had given us as a wedding gift.

I went to work on Monday morning while Billie began to ply a talent she was to repeatedly use during our lives, making wherever we lived into a genuine home. I came home to Billie and a wonderful dinner.

There are many tender memories of movies in those grand theatres of downtown Tulsa, the walks through a then vibrant downtown Tulsa window-shopping the department stores , an occasional Brown Derby at Bishop's after a movie and a payday, or late night cinnamon toast and hot chocolate at Coman's Restaurant.

TWENTY-FIVE

All the medical knowledge of 1957 had been attempted and had failed; Granddaddy came home from Mayo's Clinic that summer dying of prostate cancer. He wanted to die in his home. He had set up shop so to speak in the middle bedroom of his home, the room in which I was born and he would die

With David due in the mid of October, Billie and I moved to Stigler. I drove to school at Connors State College that fall and worked at the store. Each evening, I told him of the events at the store and took his instructions back to the store before departing for school the next morning.

Although the truth is Euless LaFave was doing a superior job of managing the store and he would take over the store during its waning years. I could not have wished for Hays and Buchanan to have been in more caring and competent hands as better roads, better cars and then Wal-Mart begin to devour the stores of such local or regional merchants.

The brief era of the store's backdoor commerce had ended, sometime between when I left in the early summer of 1955 and my return the late summer of 1957. Other cities and towns had become more hospitable, as barriers rightly fell, the need had vanished.

In one of the many almost daily conversations we would have during the coming months, we talked of his desire to be in his home.

He said, “Home has the sounds and smells of life, not the smells of sickness.” He continued, “I’m more likely to find a miracle in the smell of your grandmother’s bacon. If I need medicine, Dr. Tom will bring it.”

And supply the needed medication Dr. Tom (Conklin) did, this was a splendid rural physician; this same man who had delivered me now, in the same bedroom, oversaw my Granddaddy’s descent toward death.

Granddaddy relished the smell of Mema Mac frying bacon in the morning. I know he would have eaten bacon and tomato sandwiches as often as she would prepare them. The middle bedroom gave him access to sounds coming from the living room and the sitting room through which muted sounds from the kitchen would come. At times he would hush me so that he could hear Mema preparing dinner – the sound of pots, pans, the doors of cabinet, stove and the ice box; it never became a refrigerator in his vocabulary, and of her now quite arthritic movements about the kitchen.

Despite his increasing discomfort, he always tried to come to the table for his meals and to the living room for an evening of television. God, the man loved Red Skelton and the television that allowed him to actually see him.

Billie and “Butch”, the name Daddy had given to the unborn David, became the delights of his life. Although he had opposed any marriage before I finished college, Billie became the treasure of his last months. I do not know what they spoke of because he would only smile if I inquired. But I know she made him smile.

In the early evening of October 29, 1957, Billie went into labor. I drove the two lane road through Spiro to Fort Smith in that exotically impaired state only an intense blend fear, uncertainty and great anticipation can produce. Billie was in the front seat while mother rode in the back seat.

But the ride was only my introduction to the apprehension, the confusion and the uncertainty of child birth. St. Edward's Hospital at the time was just out of the downtown area behind the Church that sits at the end of Garrison Avenue. If there had been as many stop lights then as there are now, I would have run several of them.

But we got there and checked Billie in, Dr. Kelsey arrived and she was put in a "Labor room". Dr. Kelsey told me it would be a while and to sit with her, saying, "Don't let her get out of bed, she's going to feel like she has to go to restroom, but it is only the pressure on her bladder." And then he left us alone. I was awash in ignorance of the situation and just plain scared.

Billie was in serious labor and she wanted to go to the restroom. Now, Billie was no less determined in 1957 than she is today. But she didn't get out of the bed. And I felt horrible for having to keep her there. In the early morning hours, Dr. Kelsey came in, examined her and gave her some medication "to take the edge off the pain." About 9:00 AM on October 30, Dr. Kelsey examined her again. He told me it would still be quite a while, that Billie was resting, and I needed get something to eat.

I gathered Mother up from the waiting room and we went across the street to a drug store with a small café in it. We ate. We went back across the street and by the time we got back David had been born.

Euphoria reigned in the McBride homes of Stigler.

It seems as soon as she could, Billie with David resumed her daily visits with Granddaddy. Shortly after David's arrival, he overheard Billie in the hallway saying to David, "Let's go talk to your great-granddaddy, your Granddaddy's crazy." He repeated that story to all that would listen. I am certain Dad Bankhead, who was an almost daily visitor, heard it more times that he would care to recall.

And he loved to tell the story of one his last duck hunts with James. A case of shotgun shells came in a rather sturdy wooden box. He had a padded seat created for one end of the Remington shell case, an accommodation to the discomfort of the advancing prostate cancer. This would allow him to sit in a blind on a pond. On this hunt, James flushed three ducks, they each got one and Granddaddy shot the third out from under James. James angrily turned to him and blurted, "Granddaddy, you old fart, you shot my duck". Granddaddy loved it.

A few years later, after Granddaddy's death, Billie and I had returned to Stigler from Flagstaff for the Christmas holiday; James and I went duck hunting. We jumped 5 mallards on a pond, 3 rose my way and 2 broke to James' side. We both knocked down two; I got the third as it was flying over the dam. Then I realized that James' gun was in front of me. He was so good that he could have shot that third mallard, but he let me have the shot. I looked at him and said, "You know the old fart would have shot that duck out from under me." We both laughed until our sides literally hurt as we collected the three ducks that had hit on land, then sat on the bank and drank coffee from a thermos as the breeze carried the two ducks that had landed on the pond nearer to us and talked of Granddaddy.

I like to think we both knew there was something unique about that morning, about that shoot. We went to the house and Billie took pictures of us holding the ducks. That was the last time my brother and I were to hunt together. I still find pleasure in those pictures.

As soon as possible after David's birth, Granddaddy wanted the photograph of the four generations of McBride males taken. "I want that picture before I look like I'm dying. But he has to be old enough to sit up with us." We got the pictures with David somewhat sitting.

The late September arrival by mail of an offer of a full scholarship from Arizona State (Flagstaff) sparked a series of intense conversations between Granddaddy and me. I know that he took it as a very good omen that I had talked with Billie about this prospect before I spoke with him or anyone else. He said so.

If the offer should be accepted, Billie, David and I would have to leave immediately after Christmas. With this in mind, we had our conversations. There was a part of him that wanted me to stay in Stigler and slowly take over the store, but he also felt that improved roads would increasingly take business to Fort Smith, McAlester and Muskogee. He talked about the "new discount stores" that were emerging on the west coast, but not as a threat rather as justification to expand the collective buying with the other Hays stores. It would only be 4 years before I actually encountered a discount store in Oklahoma City.

After the housekeeping matters from the store, we would speak of the present and the future; the future of my family was of particular interest to him, while rarely going beyond an acknowledgment of the inevitability of his death, he simply was not preoccupied with his demise.

It seemed that each conversation would end with him making some kind of expression about the importance of education. His pending death was discussed only in the terms of the impact it would have on Mema Mac, while I knew they both loved me dearly, it was not until these talks that I began to comprehend how much they loved each other. It seems that he was always astounded that "a woman of her beauty" had chosen to marry a "man clerking in a store".

Only the lethal epidemic of the Hong Kong flu was to disrupt these visits. Billie and I both had it, just not at the same time. Not that there was any shortage of attention and care for young

David. Granddaddy McBride and Mema Lane had seen illness take too many children during their lifetime and both feared for David. Still even if David had contracted the disease, an illness that Granddaddy certainly could not have survived, he wanted his great-grandchild in his room. He wanted to talk to him.

TWENTY-SIX

It was not until one of our last visits that I approached the topic of the grass fire. I only ask if he had ever heard who lit our grass. He said that he had been given some names. I was somewhat surprised at this acknowledgment.

When I asked who, he said, "How would it help you to know? I found it did little good for me. Knowing most often makes a man feel like he has got to do something, when most of the times he doesn't need to. Still it can gnaw on a man."

He continued, anticipating my next question, "And the whys don't matter either, often by the time we find them out, well, they're not whys anymore. Just the whys of the moment."

My question was, "So you did nothing?"

He said, "No. When Sharpe's wouldn't let one of them have credit for school clothes, I had Dad Bankhead see that he got the word that he had credit at Hays and Buchanan if he'd come ask for it. When he came and I gave him more credit than he ask for."

"And?"

His answer came after that subtle 'I got you' smile that I can still see at times, "And he made all his payments on time."

He continued, "And there was the other one that Marshall Cooper brought to have his hand X-Rayed." "Remember?" I said I didn't.

It seems Marshall Cooper had quietly asked around and a couple of days after the fire the Marshall was visiting with a man about several gasoline cans in the bed of his pickup that smelled of kerosene. In the course of the conversation, the man placed the middle finger of his right hand into a position that got it injured.

Granddaddy said, "The Marshall thought he should bring him to the store to put his hand in the X-Ray to be certain nothing was broken. Nothing broken, likely just badly twisted."

I believe that Marshall Cooper's need to feel that he had done something was satisfied by having the man get down on his knees and stick his hand in Granddaddy's X-Ray machine. Then, consistent with Granddaddy's original wish, the good Marshall was willing to let it rest.

Granddaddy concluded, "They were just some men with too little work and too much bootleg whiskey." It had the sound of understanding without excusing the behavior.

That concluded our discussion of the matter. He never told me who they were and I never ask.

Although I believe over the preceding months we had discussed all matters he considered of value, going in to his room on the morning we left for Arizona was excruciating. I would like to think of a softer word than painful, but it was painful. It was his reassurance that made it bearable, saying, "You and Billie are doing the right thing. You listen to Billie; she's got a good head on her and got both of her feet on the ground." He preached, "Educate yourself and Butch (David) will educate himself, all your children will."

I know now hearing this theme that I had heard all my life sporadically haunted me until I completed my bachelor's degree. I am not certain why that wasn't enough, as to what drove me further to the Masters and Doctorate, but something did.

And he was absolutely correct; Billie has been not only my life's love, but also my touchstone. There are times I suspect that without her love and support, without her dogged determination, I might have actually accomplished little.

He gave me 6 stamped envelopes, preaddressed to Mr. and Mrs. J. H. McBride. He told me to write, but said that he would not be writing back. I held his hand – not a handshake – I held his hand. The skin was cool to my touch and seemed thin as tissue paper. I started to leave; I stopped at the door and took a step back toward him. I told him that I loved him. I believe that it was the only time that the word love passed between us. And then I left.

Just as we were turning onto to 7th Street, Jon Conard stepped from the curb. He and Sue had moved back to Stigler and he was operating his family nursery. They were expecting their eldest son in about the same time frame that we were expecting David. We said our goodbyes, wished each other well and I left Stigler.

TWENTY-SEVEN

Mother and Dad drove us out Highway 9 to Norman, back roads to Sayre, then Route 66 to Flagstaff. Their 1957 Plymouth station wagon towed a small borrowed trailer containing all of our possessions, which consisted of kitchen items, a crib, clothing, bedding and that little black and white Crosley television.

Billie was much more traveled that I was. It was my first time west of Oklahoma City. The change of country side as we progressed west was interesting, but not at all reassuring. It seemed a slow trip west, emphasizing the distance that was to be between us and our eastern Oklahoma roots. The unknown has a manner generating doubt. The doubts would come over me in unexpected waves; then depart as promptly as they arrived. I wondered how my classmates who had followed this path to California during their summers might have felt.

Gallup, Holbrook and Winslow were almost disturbing. Then, the snow-capped San Francisco Peaks appeared.

We arrived in Flagstaff late in the afternoon and checked into a motel near the campus. I called Coach (Herb) Gregg. He was out of town, but had left instructions with his wife that he had made all the arrangements; that I was to call the housing office. They gave me instructions and told me where the unit was, saying it was freshly painted but that it should be dry by morning.

Early the next morning, we surveyed 85 Cottage City and discovered the meaning of the term "partially furnished housing". The apartment was a living room, kitchen with small dining area, a bathroom with a shower just off the kitchen and a bedroom with 2 make-shift closets.

It was heated by a vented gas heater that sat about between the living area and the kitchen. Ultimately, the 9 x 12 rug we would put in the living room was like wall to wall carpeting. It was furnished with a twin bed in the living room, a breakfast table with 3 chairs and a double bed in the bedroom with a less than new mattress.

The reclaimed World War II married housing unit Billie and I moved into on campus in Flagstaff had just received a fresh coat of paint. This included a coat of battleship grey paint on the wooden floor.

We arrived to find setting in the middle of the floor in the area designated as the living room was a twin sized bed. There were sharp crackling sounds as we lifted it to move it against the wall. It seems that the students doing the work had painted half the room, and then lifted the twin bed onto the still sticky paint and there it stuck. We had 4 circles revealing the older paint in the middle of our fresh painted floor.

Having brought Billie and David 900 miles to a place we had never seen, in which we would be alone without extended family or even a car, my first thoughts were of concern. Billie started laughing. I saw there was delight in her eyes and I started laughing. I knew from that time on whatever the circumstances and no matter how deep we had to hunker down, we would be just fine.

And we have never lived in a place that Billie could not quickly make into our home.

In my eyes it was absolutely magnificent – and I'm not joking – I thought it was glorious. I think Billie saw it as being filled with potential. We unloaded the trailer and moved in.

The next day I had a morning and afternoon practice. While I was at the morning practice, Mother and Dad drove Billie to the grocery. While I was at the afternoon practice, Mother and Dad left to travel south to visit Boots and Jackie before returning to Stigler.

I came home just at dusky dark to find Billie playing with David on that twin bed, now covered by a bedspread, and dinner cooking. I wish I could recall what that dinner was.

It was Christmas Break at school, so the campus was basically empty. There was time between practices to walk around the campus and to walk around Flagstaff before classes began.

I used all the envelopes Granddaddy had given me except one. I know I first wrote him about the snow and of the curtains that Billie hung in the windows in the living room of 85 Cottage City. I wrote about how Billie and I would walk to the Safeway that required us to climb the high fence that divided the campus from Route 66 motels. On the way back one of us would climb the fence first, the other would pass the groceries over the fence and then follow.

Within 2 weeks, Billie found a job selling tickets at the Orpheum Theater in Flagstaff. I was really proud of her. Most nights, I would walk to the theatre, David upon my shoulders, to walk her home. I wrote him of these things.

There was the accounting of my classes in a letter because I knew above all else that was important to him. I included a description of the enrollment process that used the tables at which the instructors were seated in the gym. I never wrote that I was often writing these letters during a class.

With some reluctance, I wrote him about coming into the locker room for the first time and finding my name on the locker, two pair of new Chuck Taylor Converse All-Stars and clean practice gear neatly hung daily in the locker. I wrote of these things.

The Lumberjack Gym had a large scoreboard on the north wall on which the names and numbers of the players were placed. There was a clear light to indicate who was in the game and a set of red lights to indicate the number of fouls a player had. Before the first night I dressed for a game, I came in for an afternoon shoot around. After leaving the locker room, I had come out and started across the floor when I realized that there was a man working on the scoreboard. When I understood that he was arranging the numbers and names, that he was adding my name to the scoreboard, I stopped literally at mid-floor, the gym empty but the seating arranged for the game that evening, and watched him place the letters to spell my name on the scoreboard. It was a strange and humbling feeling, confusing in a sense. It was not the pure exhilaration I felt the first time I knelt at the scorer's table and saw the light come on by my name. I wrote him of these things.

I still remember my first basket. I over-penetrated, got jammed up with a much larger guy, recovered, got him up in the air and shot as he fell on me. It went in and I got fouled. I went to foul line, dry mouth and all, and made the foul shot.

Because I was blessed to be on a team with some truly gifted players, we won the conference championship, defeating Tucson and Tempe in the process. My teammates were so very good; I was privileged just to practice with them. Coach (Herb) Gregg was ahead of his time with the constant push of the ball, offensive and defensively. Coach Gregg took my innate competitiveness and taught me how to win.

TWENTY-EIGHT

It had snowed several inches in Flagstaff the night before. But the sun was out and the sky was clear. I had come home from a morning practice. I can't remember how I got the message to call Granddaddy's house.

I recall walking through the snow to the laundry room at the end of the building where a pay phone was located. I put my dime into the phone and placed the collect call. I forget who answered the phone, but it was passed to Uncle Elic. They had had Granddaddy's funeral that day. Uncle Elic said I hadn't been called earlier for fear I might insist on coming back. I muttered something and just hung up.

I did not need to attend his funeral or to hear the details of it from someone else to secure any type of closure; my Grandfather and I had parted in the manner of his choosing. I believe we spoke of those things that were important in our lives; certainly we spoke more of life than of death. But still I cried.

Just as I had known what the call meant, Billie also seemed to intuitively know. We talked, we cried, we played with David and we laughed. Grief is not so crippling when there is someone to share it with – I think Billie knew how much he had come to love her.

Billie walked downtown to her job at the Orpheum Theatre. Dean Resius, our Iowa neighbor in Cottage City, came over and we played cards while David napped.

Then, I bundled David and we walked to the theatre, as was our routine, so that Billie did not have to walk home alone after dark. I don't know that it was a safety issue as much as I simply enjoyed walking with her. The walk back to Cottage City on that snowy night clings to my memory, Billie and I spoke little on the walk but conversation wasn't necessary.

I was sad, but other feelings were settling firmly into place. A different sense of family, my family, was becoming so concentrated in my consciousness.

I just needed to walk home beside Billie; there were only the sounds of our feet crunching in the brittle, refrozen snow.

~

About the Author

Hal McBride was born and reared in Stigler, Oklahoma. He graduated from Stigler High School in the Class of 1955.

He received the majority of his undergraduate education at Arizona State College (now Northern Arizona University) in Flagstaff, Arizona before ultimately receiving his Bachelor's degree from Northeastern State University, Tahlequah, Oklahoma. He completed his Masters and Doctoral degrees at the University of Tulsa, Tulsa, Oklahoma.

Dr. McBride resides in Tulsa, Oklahoma with his wife, their two sons and grandchildren.

To Bear Witness is his first book.

www.ingramcontent.com/pod-product-compliance
Ingram Content Group UK Ltd.
Pitfield, Milton Keynes, MK11 3LW, UK
UKHW041941190726
13854UKWH00004B/1731